Modern Critical Interpretations

Nathaniel Hawthorne's
The Scarlet Letter

Modern Critical Interpretations

These and other titles in preparation

Modern Critical Interpretations

Nathaniel Hawthorne's
The Scarlet Letter

Edited and with an introduction by
Harold Bloom
Sterling Professor of the Humanities
Yale University

Chelsea House Publishers ◇ *1986*
NEW YORK ◇ NEW HAVEN ◇ PHILADELPHIA

Library of Congress Cataloging-in-Publication Data
Nathaniel Hawthorne's The scarlet letter.
  (Modern critical interpretations)
  Bibliography: p.
  Includes index.
  Summary: A collection of seven critical essays on
Hawthorne's novel, arranged in chronological order of original
publication.
    1. Hawthorne, Nathaniel, 1804–1864.   Scarlet letter.
[1. Hawthorne, Nathaniel, 1804–1864.   Scarlet letter.
2. American literature—History and criticism]
I. Bloom, Harold.   II. Series.
PS1868.N38 1986   813'.3   86-8316
ISBN 1-55546-005-4 (alk. paper)

Contents

Editor's Note

This book gathers together what its editor considers to be the best criticism yet published on Hawthorne's finest long fiction, *The Scarlet Letter*. The critical essays are reprinted here in the chronological order of their original publication. I am grateful to Daniel Klotz and Susan Laity for their erudition and judgment in helping to edit this volume.

My introduction isolates an antithetical strain, Emersonian and Gnostic, in the romance. In the chronological sequence that then begins, A. N. Kaul tellingly analyzes the way in which Hawthorne uses "Puritan metaphysics as a basis for the criticism of Puritan ethics." Michael J. Colacurcio's informed analysis of the relation between the historical fate of the heretic Ann Hutchinson and the fictive fate of Hester Prynne invokes a dialectic which is at once social, theological, and moral. Richard H. Brodhead's intricate account of Hawthorne's "unwillingness or inability to abjure the rough magic of romance" initiates a dialectical process that results both in aesthetic gain and aesthetic loss.

In a tribute to Hawthorne's mastery over "the humanizing power of pain," Michael Ragussis reads the romance as a mode of family discourse. Another kind of power, the non-humanizing force of "writing," is the focus of Norman Bryson's deconstruction of the scarlet letter itself.

Contemporary modes of interpreting the problematics of reading figure also in the remaining essays in this volume. Evan Carton, studying the rhetoric of American romance, argues that *The Scarlet Letter* is "about" representation. Finally, in an essay published for the first time here, Scott Derrick speculates that Hawthorne's troubled awareness of "the gender struggles of the American male artist" achieves a powerful (if shamed) Promethean apotheosis in *The Scarlet Letter*.

Introduction

Henry James's *Hawthorne* was published in December, 1879, in London, in the English Men of Letters series. Unique among the thirty-nine volumes of that group, this was a critical study of an American by an American. Only Hawthorne seemed worthy of being an English man of letters, and only James seemed capable of being an American critic. Perhaps this context inhibited James, whose *Hawthorne* tends to be absurdly overpraised, or perhaps Hawthorne caused James to feel an anxiety that even George Eliot could not bring the self-exiled American to experience. Whatever the reason, James wrote a study that requires to be read between the lines, as here in its final paragraph:

> He was a beautiful, natural, original genius, and his life had been singularly exempt from worldly preoccupations and vulgar efforts. It had been as pure, as simple, as unsophisticated, as his work. He had lived primarily in his domestic affections, which were of the tenderest kind; and then—without eagerness, without pretension, but with a great deal of quiet devotion—in his charming art. His work will remain; it is too original and exquisite to pass away; among the men of imagination he will always have his niche. No one has had just that vision of life, and no one has had a literary form that more successfully expressed his vision. He was not a moralist, and he was not simply a poet. The moralists are weightier, denser, richer, in a sense; the poets are more purely inconclusive and irresponsible. He combined in a singular degree the spontaneity of the imagination with a haunting care for moral problems. Man's conscience was his theme, but he saw it in the light of a creative fancy which added, out of its own substance, an interest, and, I may almost say, an importance.

Is *The Scarlet Letter* pure, simple, and unsophisticated? Is *The Marble Faun* a work neither moral nor poetic? Can we accurately assert that man's conscience, however lit by creative fancy, is Hawthorne's characteristic concern? James's vision of his American precursor is manifestly distorted by a need to misread creatively what may hover too close, indeed may shadow the narrative space that James requires for his own enterprise. In that space, something beyond shadowing troubles James. Isabel Archer has her clear affinities with Dorothea Brooke, yet her relation to Hester Prynne is even more familial, just as Millie Theale will have the lineage of *The Marble Faun*'s Hilda ineluctably marked upon her. James's representations of women are Hawthornian in ways subtly evasive yet finally unmistakable. Yet even this influence and its consequent ambivalences do not seem to be the prime unease that weakens James's *Hawthorne*. Rather, the critical monograph is more embarrassed than it can know by James's guilt at having abandoned the American destiny. Elsewhere, James wrote to some purpose about Emerson (though not so well as his brother William did), but in *Hawthorne* the figure of Emerson is unrecognizable and the dialectics of New England Transcendentalism are weakly abused:

> A biographer of Hawthorne might well regret that his hero had not been more mixed up with the reforming and free-thinking class, so that he might find a pretext for writing a chapter upon the state of Boston society forty years ago. A needful warrant for such regret should be, properly, that the biographer's own personal reminiscences should stretch back to that period and to the persons who animated it. This would be a guarantee of fulness of knowledge and, presumably, of kindness of tone. It is difficult to see, indeed, how the generation of which Hawthorne has given us, in *Blithedale*, a few portraits, should not, at this time of day, be spoken of very tenderly and sympathetically. If irony enter into the allusion, it should be of the lightest and gentlest. Certainly, for a brief and imperfect chronicler of these things, a writer just touching them as he passes, and who has not the advantage of having been a contemporary, there is only one possible tone. The compiler of these pages, though his recollections date only from a later period, has a memory of a certain number of persons who had been intimately connected, as Hawthorne was not, with the agitations of that interesting time. Something of its interest adhered to them still—something of its aroma clung to their garments; there was something about

them which seemed to say that when they were young and enthusiastic, they had been initiated into moral mysteries, they had played at a wonderful game. Their usual mark (it is true I can think of exceptions) was that they seemed excellently good. They appeared unstained by the world, unfamiliar with worldly desires and standards, and with those various forms of human depravity which flourish in some high phases of civilisation; inclined to simple and democratic ways, destitute of pretensions and affectations, of jealousies, of cynicisms, of snobbishness. This little epoch of fermentation has three or four drawbacks for the critics—drawbacks, however, that may be overlooked by a person for whom it has an interest of association. It bore, intellectually, the stamp of provincialism; it was a beginning without a fruition, a dawn without a noon; and it produced, with a single exception, no great talents. It produced a great deal of writing, but (always putting Hawthorne aside, as a contemporary but not a sharer) only one writer in whom the world at large has interested itself. The situation was summed up and transfigured in the admirable and exquisite Emerson. He expressed all that it contained, and a good deal more, doubtless, besides; he was the man of genius of the moment; he was the Transcendentalist *par excellence*. Emerson expressed, before all things, as was extremely natural at the hour and in the place, the value and importance of the individual, the duty of making the most of one's self, of living by one's own personal light, and carrying out one's own disposition. He reflected with beautiful irony upon the exquisite impudence of those institutions which claim to have appropriated the truth and to dole it out, in proportionate morsels, in exchange for a subscription. He talked about the beauty and dignity of life, and about every one who is born into the world being born to the whole, having an interest and a stake in the whole. He said "all that is clearly due to-day is not to lie," and a great many other things which it would be still easier to present in a ridiculous light. He insisted upon sincerity and independence and spontaneity, upon acting in harmony with one's nature, and not conforming and compromising for the sake of being more comfortable. He urged that a man should await his call, his finding the thing to do which he should really believe in doing, and not be urged by the world's opinion to do simply the world's work. "If no call

should come for years, for centuries, then I know that the want
of the Universe is the attestation of faith by my abstinence: . . .
If I cannot work, at least I need not lie." The doctrine of the
supremacy of the individual to himself, of his originality, and,
as regards his own character, *unique* quality, must have had a
great charm for people living in a society in which introspection—thanks to the want of other entertainment—played almost
the part of a social resource.

The "admirable and exquisite Emerson" was "as sweet as barbed
wire," to quote President Giamatti of Yale. Any reader of that great, grim,
and most American of books, *The Conduct of Life*, ought to have known
this. James's Emerson, dismissed here by the novelist as a provincial of real
charm, had provoked the senior Henry James to an outburst of more authentic critical value: "O you man without a handle!" Hawthorne too, in
a very different way, was a man without a handle, not less conscious and
subtle an artist than the younger Henry James himself. *The Scarlet Letter*,
in James's *Hawthorne*, is rightly called the novelist's masterpiece, but then
is accused of "a want of reality and an abuse of the fanciful element—of a
certain superficial symbolism." James was too good a reader to have indicted
Hawthorne for "a want of reality," were it not that Hawthornian representation had begun too well the process of causing a Jamesian aspect of
reality to appear.

II

Of the four principal figures in *The Scarlet Letter*, Pearl is at once the
most surprising, and the largest intimation of Hawthorne's farthest imaginings. There is no indication that Hawthorne shared his friend Melville's
deep interest in ancient Gnosticism, though esoteric heresies were clearly
part of Hawthorne's abiding concern with witchcraft. The Gnostic *Gospel
of Thomas* contains a remarkable mythic narrative, "The Hymn of the
Pearl," that juxtaposes illuminatingly with the uncanny daughter of Hester
Prynne and the Reverend Mr. Dimmesdale. In Gnostic symbolism, the
pearl is identical with the spark or *pneuma* that is the ontological self of the
adept who shares in the Gnosis, in the true knowing that surmounts mere
faith. The pearl particularly represents what is best and oldest in the adept,
because creation is the work of a mere demiurge, while the best part of us,
that which is capable of knowing, was never made, but is one with the
original Abyss, the Foremother and Forefather who is the true or alien God.
When Hawthorne's Pearl passionately insists she was not made by God,
we hear again the most ancient and challenging of all Western heresies:

The old minister seated himself in an arm-chair, and made an effort to draw Pearl betwixt his knees. But the child, unaccustomed to the touch or familiarity of any but her mother, escaped through the open window and stood on the upper step, looking like a wild, tropical bird, of rich plumage, ready to take flight into the upper air. Mr. Wilson, not a little astonished at this outbreak,—for he was a grandfatherly sort of personage, and usually a vast favorite with children,—essayed, however, to proceed with the examination.

"Pearl," said he, with great solemnity, "thou must take heed to instruction, that so, in due season, thou mayest wear in thy bosom the pearl of great price. Canst thou tell me, my child, who made thee?"

Now Pearl knew well enough who made her; for Hester Prynne, the daughter of a pious home, very soon after her talk with the child about her Heavenly Father, had begun to inform her of those truths which the human spirit, at whatever stage of immaturity, imbibes with such eager interest. Pearl, therefore, so large were the attainments of her three years' lifetime, could have borne a fair examination in the New England Primer, or the first column of the Westminster Catechism, although unacquainted with the outward form of either of those celebrated works. But that perversity, which all children have more or less of, and of which little Pearl had a tenfold portion, now, at the most inopportune moment, took thorough possession of her, and closed her lips, or impelled her to speak words amiss. After putting her finger in her mouth, with many ungracious refusals to answer good Mr. Wilson's question, the child finally announced that she had not been made at all, but had been plucked by her mother off the bush of wild roses, that grew by the prison-door.

That Pearl, elf-child, is the romance's prime knower no reader would doubt. The subtlest relation in Hawthorne's sinuously ambiguous romance is not that between Chillingworth and Dimmesdale, let alone the inadequate ghost of the love between Hester and Dimmesdale. It is the ambivalent and persuasive mother–daughter complex in which Hester is saved both from suicidal despair and from the potential of becoming the prophetess of a feminist religion only by the extraordinary return in her daughter of everything she herself has repressed. I will venture the speculation that both Hester and Pearl are intense representations of two very different aspects of Emersonianism, Hester being a prime instance of Emerson's American religion of self-reliance, while Pearl emerges from a deeper stratum of Emerson, from the Orphism and Gnosticism that mark the sage's first anarchic influx of power and knowledge, when he celebrated his own version of what he called, following the Swedenborgians, the terrible freedom or newness. Emerson, Hawthorne's Concord walking companion, is generally judged by scholars and critics to be antithetical to Hawthorne. I doubt that judgment, since manifestly Hawthorne does not prefer the pathetic Dimmesdale and the mock-satanic Chillingworth to the self-reliant Hester and the daemonic Pearl. Henry James, like T. S. Eliot, considered Emerson to be deficient in a sense of sin, a sense obsessive in Dimmesdale and Chillingworth, alien to Pearl, and highly dialectical in Hester.

In the Gnostic mode of Pearl, the young Emerson indeed affirmed: "My heart did never counsel me to sin. . . . /I never taught it what it teaches me." This is the adept of Orphic mysteries who also wrote: "It is God in you that responds to God without, or affirms his own words trembling on the lips of another," words that "sound to you as old as yourself." The direct precursor to *The Scarlet Letter*'s Pearl is a famous moment in Emerson's "Self-Reliance," an essay surely known to Hawthorne:

> I remember an answer which when quite young I was prompted to make to a valued adviser who was wont to importune me with the dear old doctrines of the church. On my saying, "What have I to do with the sacredness of traditions, if I live wholly from within?" my friend suggested,—"But these impulses may be from below, not from above." I replied, "They do not seem to me to be such; but if I am the Devil's child, I will live then from the Devil."

Call this Pearl's implicit credo, since her positive declaration is: "I have no Heavenly Father!" Even as Pearl embodies Emerson's most anarchic, antinomian strain, Hester incarnates the central impulse of "Self-Reliance." This is the emphasis of chapter 13 of the romance, "Another View of Hester," which eloquently tells us: "The scarlet letter had not done its office." In effect, Hawthorne presents her as Emerson's American precursor, and as the forerunner also of movements still working themselves through among us:

> Much of the marble coldness of Hester's impression was to be attributed to the circumstance that her life had turned, in a great measure, from passion and feeling, to thought. Standing alone in the world,—alone, as to any dependence on society, and with

little Pearl to be guided and protected,—alone, and hopeless of retrieving her position, even had she not scorned to consider it desirable,—she cast away the fragments of a broken chain. The world's law was no law for her mind. It was an age in which the human intellect, newly emancipated, had taken a more active and a wider range than for many centuries before. Men of the sword had overthrown nobles and kings. Men bolder than these had overthrown and rearranged—not actually, but within the sphere of theory, which was their most real abode—the whole system of ancient prejudice, wherewith was linked much of ancient principle. Hester Prynne imbibed this spirit. She assumed a freedom of speculation, then common enough on the other side of the Atlantic, but which our forefathers, had they known of it, would have held to be a deadlier crime than that stigmatized by the scarlet letter. In her lonesome cottage, by the sea-shore, thoughts visited her, such as dared to enter no other dwelling in New England; shadowy guests, that would have been as perilous as demons to their entertainer, could they have been seen so much as knocking at her door.

It is remarkable, that persons who speculate the most boldly often conform with the most perfect quietude to the external regulations of society. The thought suffices them, without investing itself in the flesh and blood of action. So it seemed to be with Hester. Yet, had little Pearl never come to her from the spiritual world, it might have been far otherwise. Then, she might have come down to us in history, hand in hand with Ann Hutchinson, as the foundress of a religious sect. She might, in one of her phases, have been a prophetess. She might, and not improbably would, have suffered death from the stern tribunals of the period, for attempting to undermine the foundations of the Puritan establishment. But, in the education of her child, the mother's enthusiasm of thought had something to wreak itself upon. Providence, in the person of this little girl, had assigned to Hester's charge the germ and blossom of womanhood, to be cherished and developed amid a host of difficulties. Every thing was against her. The world was hostile. The child's own nature had something wrong in it, which continually betokened that she had been born amiss,—the effluence of her mother's lawless passion,—and often impelled Hester to ask, in bitterness of heart, whether it were for ill or good that the poor little creature had been born at all.

Indeed, the same dark question often rose into her mind, with reference to the whole race of womanhood. Was existence worth accepting, even to the happiest among them? As concerned her own individual existence, she had long ago decided in the negative, and dismissed the point as settled. A tendency to speculation, though it may keep woman quiet, as it does man, yet makes her sad. She discerns, it may be, such a hopeless task before her. As a first step, the whole system of society is to be torn down, and built up anew. Then, the very nature of the opposite sex, or its long hereditary habit, which has become like nature, is to be essentially modified, before woman can be allowed to assume what seems a fair and suitable position. Finally, all other difficulties being obviated, woman cannot take advantage of these preliminary reforms, until she herself shall have undergone a still mightier change; in which, perhaps, the ethereal essence, wherein she has her truest life, will be found to have evaporated. A woman never overcomes these problems by any exercise of thought. They are not to be solved, or only in one way. If her heart chance to come uppermost, they vanish. Thus, Hester Prynne, whose heart had lost its regular and healthy throb, wandered without a clew in the dark labyrinth of mind; now turned aside by an insurmountable precipice; now starting back from a deep chasm. There was wild and ghastly scenery all around her, and a home and comfort nowhere. At times, a fearful doubt strove to possess her soul, whether it were not better to send Pearl at once to heaven, and go herself to such futurity as Eternal Justice should provide.

Only the emanation of Pearl from the spiritual world has saved Hester from the martyrdom of a prophetess, which is Hawthorne's most cunning irony, since without Pearl his romance would have been transformed into a tragedy. That may be our loss, aesthetically, since every reader of *The Scarlet Letter* comes to feel a great regret at Hester's unfulfilled potential. Something in us wants her to be a greater heretic even than Ann Hutchinson. Certainly we sense an unwritten book in her, a story that Hawthorne did not choose to write. But what he had written marks the true beginning of American prose fiction, the absolute point of origin from which we can trace the sequence that goes from Melville and James to Faulkner and Pynchon and that domesticates great narrative art in America.

The Scarlet Letter
and Puritan Ethics

A. N. Kaul

In reading *The Scarlet Letter* it is necessary to remember that this is a book about and not of seventeenth-century New England. There is a danger, that is to say, of confusing the subject of the novel with the novelist's attitude, especially because the latter involves an irony which often assumes the innocent guise of approval. In many ways Hawthorne was undoubtedly the heir of the Puritan tradition, but he was also one of its severest critics. His criticism, more searching and sustained than that of Fenimore Cooper before him, has at times the damaging effectiveness, without the invective, of the Smart Set's guerilla attacks in the twentieth century. For instance, his comment on the portraits in Governor Bellingham's house—"as if they were the ghosts, rather than the pictures, of departed worthies, and were gazing with harsh and intolerant criticism at the pursuits and enjoyments of living men"—recalls Mencken's quick-fire definition of Puritanism as "the haunting fear that someone, somewhere may be happy." One can also see in the description of the Puritan children's two favorite pastimes of playing at going to church and scalping Indians, a parallel to the jest that the Pilgrim Fathers first fell upon their knees and then upon the aborigines. Unlike Cooper, Hawthorne never made the fate of the Indians his theme, but all the same, like the older writer, he felt and often expressed a sense of compassion for the depredations suffered by that race. To take the most striking example, this feeling enters poignantly the account of the history of American civilization, as Hawthorne gives it in "Main Street," finding

From *The American Vision: Actual and Ideal Society in Nineteenth-Century Fiction.*
© 1963 by Yale University. Yale University Press, 1963. Originally entitled
"Nathaniel Hawthorne: Heir and Critic of the Puritan Tradition."

a climax in the terse observation: "The pavements of the Main Street must be laid over the red man's grave." The same sketch, however, offers the well-known and more balanced statement of Hawthorne's attitude toward the American Puritans: "Let us thank God for having given us such ancestors; and let each successive generation thank Him, not less fervently, for being one step further from them in the march of ages."

Hawthorne himself was several thankful generations away from the Pilgrim Fathers. Actually he lived in the same generation with Emerson. But to state in this manner the distance that separates him from the subject of his novel can be misleading. Unlike Emerson, he was not cut off from the Puritans by the impassable peak of a novel and exciting theory of the cosmos. Nor did he view them as Cooper did—across the limitless spaces of the Hudson River. His attitude toward his subject suggests a complex relation rather than an intractable and artistically sterile distance. On account of his personal temperament, his artistic sensibility, and his family history, he could approach the seventeenth century as an insider, retaining at the same time the outsider's ability and freedom to judge and evaluate. Like so many great works of literature—Arthur Koestler's *Darkness at Noon* is a notable modern example—*The Scarlet Letter* is a searching criticism of the world with which it deals precisely because it takes its stand firmly within that world.

Consider, for example, the central fact around which Hawthorne builds the curious pattern of his novel. The all-pervasive sense of sin is as important here as it was in the life and thought of the first Puritans. But we must not forget on the other hand that the artist who evokes it is a man of radically different sympathies, the author, among other things, of "The New Adam and Eve." There is a passage in this story which it is worthwhile to cite in detail because it provides an explicit statement of the attitude that shapes the moral action of *The Scarlet Letter*. I am referring to the passage where, during their puzzled wandering through the landmarks of old humanity, the precursors of the new order arrive at an edifice which is described as both a prison and a hospital, serving as an emblem of that attitude of punitive correction toward sinners which was the hallmark of Puritan polity. The prisonhouse is now deserted because the Day of Judgment has swept all human beings from the face of the earth and "a new trial has been granted in a higher court which may set judge, jury, and prisoner at its bar all in a row, and perhaps find one no less guilty than another." The new Adam and Eve, "so fresh from their Creator's hand," stand baffled before the mystery of this edifice. They have no means of discovering that it was

a hospital for the direst disease which could afflict their predecessors. Its patients bore the outward marks of that leprosy with
which all were more or less infected. They were sick—and so
were the purest of their brethren—with the plague of sin. A
deadly sickness, indeed! Feeling its symptoms within the breast,
men concealed it with fear and shame, and were only the more
cruel to those unfortunates whose pestiferous sores were flagrant
to the common eye. Nothing save a rich garment could ever
hide the plague spot. In the course of the world's lifetime, every
remedy was tried for its cure and extirpation except the single
one, the flower that grew in heaven and was sovereign for all
the miseries of earth. Man never had attempted to cure sin by
Love. Had he but once made the effort it might well have happened that there would have been no more need of the dark lazar
house into which Adam and Eve have wandered.

This direct authorial comment can serve as a preface to Hawthorne's
image of seventeenth-century New England society in *The Scarlet Letter*.
One can, moreover, see the age to which such a comment belongs by
setting beside it the following statement from Emerson's "Man the Reformer": "This great, overgrown, dead Christendom of ours still keeps
alive at least the name of a lover of mankind. But one day all men will be
lovers; and every calamity will be dissolved in the universal sunshine." Of
course, the effectiveness of Hawthorne's novel arises not from any general
doctrine but from the rich particularity with which he explores a definite
historical phase of society as well as the fate of individuals in it. It is
characteristic of his temper and times again, however, that he should set
out on his evaluation of the Puritan settlement by conceding its importance
as a utopian experiment. "The founders of a new colony," we read on the
first page of the novel, "whatever utopia of human virtue and happiness
they might originally project, have invariably recognized it among their
earliest practical necessities to allot a portion of the virgin soil as a cemetery,
and another portion as the site of a prison."

   This seeming concession, however, strikes also the first note of Hawthorne's criticism. The prison in the action of the novel, as in "The New
Adam and Eve," being a place for the correction of sinners, the point of
Hawthorne's irony in linking it with the cemetery is not to deny the belief
in the inevitability of sin but rather to endorse it, and thereby to focus his
concern wholly on the problem of human response to this central fact of

life. Here as elsewhere, then, Hawthorne is using Puritan metaphysics as a basis for the criticism of Puritan ethics. What *The Scarlet Letter* calls in question is a scheme of regeneration which on the one hand allots to sin the universal status of death and on the other reserves for it the special shame of the prisonhouse. In this novel, as much as in *The Blithedale Romance*, Hawthorne does not oppose the given theory by an alternative theory of his own. His method in each case is to make the theory double up on itself by proposing to it the test of a crucial human situation which falls well within its assumptions. *L'affaire Hester* becomes thus the appropriate test for seventeenth-century New England: the case of a fallen woman brought before the tribunal of a community which believes all humanity fallen. One does not have to go to "Young Goodman Brown" to see the critical use Hawthorne makes of the Puritan belief in universal sin. Toward the end of *The Scarlet Letter*, he observes that Dimmesdale's dying in the arms of a sinful woman had struck his admirers as a noble gesture, a way of demonstrating to the world "how utterly nugatory is the choicest of man's own righteousness," a parable enacted by the man of God to impress on the people "the mighty and mournful lesson, that, in the view of Infinite Purity, we are sinners all alike." But the incredulity of these witnesses with regard to the true nature of Dimmesdale's action is not surprising, for, as Hawthorne says earlier in the novel: "The sainted minister in the church! The woman of the scarlet letter in the market-place! What imagination would have been irreverent enough to surmise that the same scorching stigma was on them both!" The irony of the situation is that the noble parable of theory should be the shameful fact of life, that the obvious implications of the lesson should be so disregarded in practice, and that the divine insight into the impossibility of human righteousness should lead not to a sense of humility but to bigoted self-righteousness and moral blindness.

Nor does the bond of sin extend only to the chief personages in the drama. It unites likewise all the members of the community. "Had Hester sinned alone?" Hawthorne asks in chapter 5, and goes on to describe how, though she struggles against such mysterious power, Hester's experience has given her the ability to recognize fellow sinners instinctively, and how, in token of such recognition, the emblem of sin on her bosom throbs sympathetically in the presence of magistrate, minister, sanctified matron, and spotless maiden alike. Hawthorne's criticism, at times muted and at others rising into open denunciation and satire, is directed fundamentally against the denial of this innate sense of human communion. If sin is the postulated basis of life, should its open manifestation be treated with understanding and compassion or with inhuman chastisement? The answer of the Puritan community to this question—posed concretely in their midst by Hester—is to put her upon the pillory, to make her bear permanently the stigma of her shame, and finally to excommunicate her. The most terrible part, the truly inhuman aspect, of Hester's fate is not that she is punished publicly but that her punishment takes the form of isolating her from the rest of the community. Even while she is standing in the center of the crowd in the marketplace, the letter *A* has "the effect of a spell, taking her out of the ordinary relations with humanity, and enclosing her in a sphere by herself."

The Scarlet Letter presents thus a highly complex variation on Hawthorne's general theme of human isolation and human community. In the drama of society and solitude which is enacted here, there is no doubt about the side on which the novel aligns our sympathies. Hester Prynne's isolation is inflicted upon her rather than willfully sought by her; and if it does not warp her moral personality, the reason is that she seeks throughout her life to reestablish a relationship with other human beings on a new and more honest basis—in other words, she is isolated by society but not alienated from humanity. The blame for her tragic predicament falls heavily on the Puritan arbiters of her destiny. Even in terms of their own stern theory of sin, her excommunication, if one uses the metaphor of "The New Adam and Eve," amounts to the banishment of a leper from a leper colony. But in reality the author's judgment of Hester is very different from that of the Puritan community. While not disputing the sinfulness of her deed, he presents her also as a source of new life and moral vitality and as a woman of the tenderest human sympathies in a cold and intolerant society. He provides her adultery with a background of long bondage in a loveless marriage, and invests the passion which leads to it with "a consecration of its own."

Hawthorne, in fact, uses the very symbol with which society identifies Hester, as a means of reversing its view of her. To the Puritans, with their allegorical habit of mind and their interpretation of life as though it were a Morality play, the meaning of the *A* is clear. But not so to a humane critic of the Puritan view of life. In an allegory the hidden meaning is easy to discover; indeed it is the allegory itself which superficially conceals it. The purpose of allegory is to strengthen, by an exercise of fancy, the received doctrine and the shared moral code. Symbols, on the contrary, put accepted meanings into doubt, introduce new ones, and finally create a radically different alignment of sympathies. Thus, while Hester becomes the sympathetic heroine of the novel, the society which persecutes her is revealed as not only bigoted and joyless but essentially evil; for to it belongs, equally with Chillingworth but without Chillingworth's personal justification, the unpardonable sin of violating in cold blood the sanctity of a human heart. Such indeed is the moral import of the inquisitorial scenes in the marketplace where the entire community has assembled to make a public spectacle of Hester's private sin. The iron-visaged good women of the settlement pour malice and abuse on her. The grim beadle, who leads her to the pillory through the remorseless crowd, calls down a "blessing on the righteous Colony of the Massachusetts, where iniquity is dragged out into the sunshine!" And, as for the governor, the magistrates, and the ministers, "out of the whole human family, it would not have been easy to select the same number of wise and virtuous persons, who should be less capable of sitting in judgment on an erring woman's heart, and disentangling its mesh of good and evil, than the sages of rigid aspect towards whom Hester Prynne now turned her face. She seemed conscious, indeed, that whatever sympathy she might expect lay in the larger and warmer heart of the multitude." Not one of these judges sees any virtue in her refusal to reveal the name of her lover. Even the kindly old John Wilson berates this token of her loyalty as unregenerate hardness and obstinacy; while the unrecognized lover himself, with curious moral hypocrisy, calls upon her from his elevated stand with the other dignitaries, to denounce the companion of her sin and not deny to him "the bitter, but wholesome, cup that is now presented to thy lips!" The effect of the scene — of its cruelty and the general absence of pity and understanding in it—is heightened rather than dispelled by the occasional soft words of the young mother, the one sympathetic observer in the hostile crowd, who tries ineffectually to remind her neighbors that Hester's suffering does not need this added inhumanity to make it an adequate atonement for her sin.

Here, then, planted at the outset of the novel, is Hawthorne's image of New England society, a society which claimed to have based itself on the highest principles of moral idealism but which turns out at the first test to be utterly lacking in the elementary Christian virtues of love and compassion. Its program of regeneration is in reality a mask for repression, and its intolerance and bigotry are worse than those of the European society from which it has, on that very account, separated itself. What its rulers seek assiduously is not the establishment of a republic of brotherly love but rather ruthless power over men. Their hypocrisy, the consequence of the wide divergence between their ideals and the practical aims of their enterprise, is insinuated everywhere, most strikingly in the contrast between the Puritan profession of austerity and the magnificence of the governor's residence which "might have befitted Aladdin's palace, rather than the mansion of a grave old Puritan ruler." Rich garments too are "readily allowed to individuals dignified by rank or wealth, even while sumptuary laws forbade these and similar extravagances to the plebeian order." This is indeed not the proclaimed city upon the hill—the refuge and sanctuary of oppressed generations and the future hope of mankind. On the contrary, the true hope of humanity lies in seeking refuge from rather than in it. "Begin all anew!" as Hester urges Dimmesdale in the forest. "Hast thou exhausted possibility in the failure of this one trial? Not so! The future is yet full of trial and success. There is happiness to be enjoyed! There is good to be done! Exchange this false life of thine for a true one."

The challenge to break away from organized society is there in Hawthorne as much as in Cooper. It provides the backbone of the dramatic conflict in *The Scarlet Letter*. That this challenge is not successfully executed is due to what one can only call Hawthorne's greater historical and psychological realism—a realism which recognizes that the protagonists, Dimmesdale particularly, are themselves encumbered with the spirit of that same society against which they find themselves in rebellion. This is a tragic novel which ends in failure, waste, and death but which, like all true tragedies, affirms the very values that go down in defeat. That moral victory belongs to Hester. The future she talks about so passionately in the passage I have cited above is of course primarily her own domestic future. But nevertheless she comes to understand that such a future is intimately connected with the future of the whole society, and that true relationships cannot exist in the family unless they are also established in the civil community at large.

Hester's unavailing attempt to reconstruct her life forms the substance of the novel's action after her banishment from society. Although she is free to leave the colony altogether, she does not do so, but instead takes her stand at the farthest edge of the settlement. The reason for this, as given in chapter 5, is twofold. In the first place, while society has cast her off, she herself has not lost hold of the magnetic chain of humanity: "The chain that bound her here was of iron links, and galling to her inmost soul, but could never be broken." The deeper reason—the reason which, with her own consciousness of sin, she trembles to acknowledge even to herself— lies in the more intimate bond of love. "There dwelt, there trode the feet of one with whom she deemed herself connected in a union, that, unrecognized on earth, would bring them together before the bar of final judgment." Her relationship with the civil community is perforce of a marginal character. Being an outcast, and with her own judgment of society's institutions, she neither seeks nor is allowed a full place in it. Whether as a skillful embroiderer or a sister of mercy at scenes of grief and misfortune, her attitude is one of unobtrusive and undemanding sympathy. She is charitable to all alike, though, as Hawthorne says, the recipients of her kindness often bit the hand from which they received it.

By far the more interesting part of the novel, however, deals with the story within the story: the drama of broken family relationships within the larger drama of the protagonist's relation to society. The remarkable thing about the structure of *The Scarlet Letter* is the controlled integration of these two aspects of the theme, and the manner in which it connects the dominant principles of one sphere with the failure of human relationship in the other. The broken circuit of the family community thus reflects the absence of the magnetic chain of love and compassion in the civil community. The inner drama itself is accordingly enacted on two different scenes: the public stage of the marketplace and the more private one of the forest; the uniformly spaced actions on the scaffold of the pillory paralleling the short, consecutive chapters which describe first Hester and Pearl, then Hester and Dimmesdale, and finally all three together in the primeval woods. Of the two characters intimately bound up with Hester, Arthur Dimmesdale, the key figure in the tragedy of her personal life, is wholly committed to the public order which has banished her; while Pearl, the born outcast of society, owns no allegiance except to the private law of family affections. Between themselves they represent the two sides of the heroine's tragically divided world. It is a conflict whose development makes Pearl the final judgment on Dimmesdale and the society to which he belongs, even as she finally becomes the one solace of Hester's life. To Hester herself comes not happiness but the gift of understanding through pain and suffering.

During the first pillory scene, Pearl, true to the law which has brought her into existence, holds up her hand plaintively toward Dimmesdale, who, removed from the mother and child, is ensconced upon the seat of judgment. If in the conflict thus dramatized the minister is disloyal to the family community, it is not entirely from fear of the social establishment. His cowardice—the "anguish of pusillanimity," as Henry James calls it—arises rather from the workings of the Puritan order within his own consciousness. His sense of personal sin is overwhelming to the point of moral blindness. By keeping him from joining Hester and Pearl on the public scaffold, it leads him to add hypocrisy and falseness to sin. In him we find again that morbid concern with self, that unrighteous egotism, which evades all issues of human responsibility by subtly transferring them to some clandestine register maintained between God and the individual soul. "He thus typified the constant introspection wherewith he tortured, but could not purify, himself." Because he is false to his primary social duty, because he is oblivious of his duty to Hester and Pearl—because, in short, he has withdrawn into himself and lost hold of the chain of human relationships—his is the inevitable fate reserved for such action in Hawthorne's universe: the whole world seems to him false, even nonexistent, and he himself "becomes a shadow, or, indeed, ceases to exist."

It is to escape the torture of such feeling that Dimmesdale ascends the pillory one night under cover of darkness. When Hester and Pearl join him and the three stand holding hands, it seems as if "the mother and the child were communicating their vital warmth to his half-torpid system. The three formed an electric chain." However, "subtle, but remorseful hypocrite" that he is, he knows that his action will remain as hidden from the world as his sin. Being committed so deeply to the society from which he is hiding his true self, there can be no redemption for him unless his confession is as public as Hester's had been earlier. "Thou wast not bold!—thou wast not true!" as Pearl mockingly reminds him. "Thou wouldst not promise to take my hand, and mother's hand, to-morrow noontide!"

This is the background one must keep in mind while approaching the magnificent forest scenes in the novel. Hester's action in seeking an interview with Dimmesdale is prompted primarily by her concern for his almost complete disintegration. Her compassion and loyalty, her taking the blame for his wretchedness upon herself, are in sharp contrast with his total self-absorption. She is compassionate even to Chillingworth who, it must be said, rewards her at least with ample understanding and a certain measure of sympathy. However, although her initial purpose is only to acquaint her lover with the true identity of Roger Chillingworth, the manner in which these scenes develop—and the human challenge that is developed with them—makes *The Scarlet Letter* a tragedy rather than simply a tale of unrelieved suffering. It is here too that Hester attains the full stature of a tragic heroine, who suffers, to be sure, but suffers with spirit and not entirely without hope. Her courage and vitality revive Dimmesdale from his long period of spiritual and moral numbness. With the insight and freedom she has so painfully won, she succeeds in relieving her lover from the torture of his morbid apprehensions, both of this world and the next, and in showing him the true path to redemption. "Heaven would show mercy," she says, "hadst thou but the strength to take advantage of it." And, as for the dreaded settlement and the men of iron who inhabit it: "Is the world, then, so narrow?" There is the pathless wilderness or the broad pathway of the sea—either of which will lead them to a new freedom.

The important thing here is to realize how fully the novel aligns our sympathies with Hester, and how completely it endorses, as a means of both heavenly and earthly redemption, her plan of withdrawing from the stern Puritan colony. As soon as the decision is made, Dimmesdale feels an unaccustomed sense of exhilaration, while Hester's beauty reappears in all its oriental splendor.

> And, as if the gloom of the earth and sky had been but the effluence of these two mortal hearts, it vanished with their sorrow. All at once, as with a sudden smile of heaven, forth burst the sunshine, pouring a very flood into the obscure forest, gladdening each green leaf, transmuting the yellow fallen ones to gold, and gleaming adown the gray trunks of the solemn trees. The objects that had made a shadow hitherto, embodied the brightness now. The course of the little brook might be traced by its merry gleam afar into the wood's heart of mystery, which had become a mystery of joy.

It is interesting to read this scene in the light of Emerson's statement (quoted earlier) contrasting dead Christendom with the universal sunshine of love. Nor must we forget the metaphorical meaning of sunshine in Hawthorne's own tales: its association with eternity in "The Minister's Black Veil" and, in "Egotism," its being the type of "the radiance of the Creator's face, expressing his love for all the creatures of his hand."

The ambiguity of Hawthorne's treatment of the forest reflects, as in the case of the scarlet *A*, the divergence between possible attitudes toward it. In itself, as is obvious from the passage quoted above, it possesses no predetermined character, either for good or for evil. It is a moral *tabula rasa*. As Hawthorne says a little later while speaking of Pearl: "The great black forest—stern as it showed itself to those who brought the guilt and troubles of the world into its bosom—became the playmate of the lonely infant, as well as it knew how." To the Puritans it appears undoubtedly a dark and gloomy place, but that is only a reflection of their own confined and joyless view of life, for, as Hawthorne says in an earlier chapter in describing Pearl's fanciful personification of natural objects to people her solitary existence: "The pine-trees, aged, black, and solemn, and flinging groans and other melancholy utterances on the breeze, needed little transformation to figure as Puritan elders." To the lovers, on the other hand, the forest provides a blissful prospect of refuge, just as the brook, mournful under the shade of Puritan gloom, symbolizes to them the joyful mystery of life.

The lawless wilderness is thus lawless only insofar as it is beyond the reach of the established law. To the little family community seeking to flee the intolerant Puritan society, it is what it had earlier been to the Puritans themselves: a haven of freedom and the possibility of starting a new life. That Hester and Dimmesdale finally choose the other alternative, the alternative of going back to the comparative freedom which even the Old World offers, is because in view of Dimmesdale's weak health they judge it more suitable than the hazardous task of working among the Indians in the wilderness. But the possibility of escape remains only a possibility. And it is just as well: to start a new life in the world there must first be born a new moral consciousness. Hester and Dimmesdale are far from being the Adam and Eve of a new order. Dimmesdale belongs wholly to the faith whose "pressure" is essential to his peace, "supporting, while it confined him within its iron framework." Unlike Hester, he has not undergone any "experience calculated to lead him beyond the scope of generally received laws . . . At the head of the social system, as the clergymen of that day stood, he was only the more trammelled by its regulations, its principles, and even its prejudices." He certainly is not the man to take advantage of either Heaven's or Hester's proffered mercy. The challenge of her plan, for all his temporary sense of exhilaration and freedom, has in effect a further disintegrating influence upon him. In contrast with her revived hope and firm dignity, his behavior during the walk back to the settlement is that of a man whose outlook on life has been not altered but merely unsettled. After years of sanctimonious piety he suddenly lapses into needless and blasphemous profanity. When Hester sees him again after the secret interview, he has reverted to his old self. Marching at the head of the procession, "he seemed so remote from her own sphere, and utterly beyond her reach . . . so unattainable in his worldly position, and still more so in that far vista of his unsympathizing thoughts, through which she now beheld him! Her spirit sank with the idea that all must have been a delusion, and that, vividly as she had dreamed it, there could be no real bond betwixt the clergyman and herself." The one thought of "this exemplary man," wholly self-absorbed again, is to preach the Election Sermon so well that the world may say of him ever after that he left "no public duty unperformed, nor ill performed!" In short, after resolving, like Huckleberry Finn, to go to hell rather than desert his loyalty to the private world—which is also his foremost moral duty—Dimmesdale returns piously to die on the public and well-beaten road to heaven.

The Scarlet Letter is a profound comment on the breakdown of human relationships in the society of the seventeenth century—a society which perhaps carried the seed of the dislocations more readily observable in our own. The force of individualism, which exerted itself on many spheres of experience, was at once its special glory and the cause of alienating man from man in it. Moreover, whether or not it was the age of dissociated sensibility, as presented in *The Scarlet Letter*, it reveals the beginnings of a disintegration in the individual psyche: a tendency for the life of the body, the mind, and the soul to fall apart, somewhat like the broken and isolated lives of Hester, Chillingworth, and Dimmesdale. There is in it a lack of that wholeness of life which Emerson took for his theme in "The American Scholar" and which has been noted more recently by W. B. Yeats in the following lines of his "Among School Children":

> Labour is blossoming or dancing where
> The body is not bruised to pleasure soul,
> Nor beauty born out of its own despair,
> Nor blear-eyed wisdom out of midnight oil.

It is a measure of Hawthorne's historical and psychological insight that he recognized that the effort to achieve a well-integrated community life in such a world must lead to tragedy. The social principles of the Puritans, laudable in their idealism, become in reality a travesty of Christian aspirations. Hester's attempt to achieve a more wholesome family community ends in failure. What is left at the conclusion of the novel is a vague hope that, with her father's public acknowledgment of her, the curse is lifted from Pearl's alienated existence, and that in some distant land she "would grow up amid human joy and sorrow, nor forever do battle with the world, but be a woman in it." She will realize, in other words, the future that Hester had dreamed of in her interview with Dimmesdale. As for the tragic heroine herself, she gains the understanding that love cannot come to fruition in a world divided against itself, that the fortunes of the family community are intimately bound up with the character of the civil community in which it exists, and that, for the full realization of human happiness: "As a first step, the whole system of society is to be torn down, and built up anew."

Footsteps of Ann Hutchinson:
The Context of *The Scarlet Letter*

Michael J. Colacurcio

The place to begin an exploration of the inner similarities between Hester Prynne and Ann Hutchinson is with a closer look at Hawthorne's early sketch ["Mrs. Hutchinson"]. In many ways a puzzling piece of historical fiction, the sketch does clear up one fundamental point immediately: Hester's sexual problems can be related to those of Mrs. Hutchinson because the latter are, in Hawthorne's view, themselves flagrantly sexual.

The sketch introduces itself, too heavily, as a lesson in that forlorn subject we used to call the nature and place of women. Mrs. Hutchinson is first presented as "the female"; she is offered as a forerunner of certain nameless public ladies of 1830, and the line from Hawthorne's remark here about "how much of the texture and body of cisatlantic literature is the work of those slender fingers" to the more famous but equally sexist one later about "the damned mob of scribbling women" seems to run direct. The revelation is damaging enough, but fairly simple: Hawthorne enjoyed competing with women for the readership of magazines and gift books at the outset of his career as little as he did for the "gentle reader" of romances later.

But if Hawthorne's own sexual politics are easy and largely irrelevant to the present question, certain subtler forms of the feminist problem treated in "Mrs. Hutchinson" throw an important light on Hester Prynne (as well as on a significant woman-problem in Hawthorne's larger career). Once we read on and apprehend Hawthorne's dominant image of Ann Hutch-

From *ELH* 39, no. 3 (September 1972). © 1972 by The Johns Hopkins University Press.

inson—formerly a spiritual counsellor to Puritan women, interpreting to them the best of the male theological mind; now a prophet in her own right, giving voice to a new spirit of freedom and embodying within herself a new awareness of female intelligence and social power—we immediately grasp the significant context of Hawthorne's views of the later Hester Prynne.

In the epilogue which Hawthorne calls a "Conclusion," Hester has returned to Boston to wear her scarlet letter "of her own free will," with something like an internalized acceptance of its appropriateness. She now accepts as reasonable what in the forest she tried to deny and many years earlier she could, in very much the same words, only rationalize: "Here had been her sin; here, her sorrow; and here was yet to be her penitence." But this is not the whole story. Whether to affirm a yet undestroyed inner-direction and unreconstructed self-reliance, or else to assert once again the mortal irreparability of ruined walls, the narrator informs us that Hester is still a visionary and has become a counsellor to women. Earlier—even in her most antinomian moments—she had stopped short of that critical move from undisciplined private speculation to unsanctioned public prophecy; providentially she had been prevented from joining hands (metaphorically) with her sister Hutchinson because "in the education of the child, the mother's enthusiasm of thought had something to wreak itself upon." Now, although Hester has apparently picked up and pieced together again "the fragments of [the] broken chain" formerly cast away; although "the world's law" is now apparently *some* law to her mind; and although she would not now presumably claim for her adultery a totally sufficient "consecration" in feeling, she has now found a way to make public her ideas about sexual justice.

Earlier she had pondered the "dark question" of the "whole race of womanhood": could its lot ever be a happy one without a tearing down of "the whole system of society" and an essential modification of "the very nature of the opposite sex?" Now—with important modifications of tone and in separation from all traces of antinomian self-justification—her ideas are expressed to other women, especially those whose lives have been made miserable through excess or absence of passion.

> Hester comforted and counseled them, as best she might. She assured them, too, of her firm belief, that, at some brighter period, when the world should have grown ripe for it, in Heaven's own time, a new truth would be revealed, in order to establish the whole relation between man and woman on a surer ground of mutual happiness.

What Hester's experience comes to finally—in an epilogue, and after a painful and complicated development forced upon her by others—is some insight about the double standard, or perhaps about the new morality.

Thus, if we can bear the temporary critical reduction, it is easy to see that Hester passes through a phase of antinomianism comparable to (though not identical with) that of the historical Ann Hutchinson, only to emerge as a version of the sexual reformer already "typed out" in Hawthorne's "figure" of Mrs. Hutchinson as independent and reforming "female." And though the equation might need to be clarified by an examination of the precise quality of Hester's anti-legal phase, we can already calculate that her final position is, in Hawthorne's mental universe, just about half way between Ann Hutchinson and Margaret Fuller; and we can sense that when Hawthorne describes her later career as counsellor to troubled and searching women, he has certain seventeenth-century, Sunday-evening doctrinal meetings and certain nineteenth-century "Conversations" just about equally in mind. (What this clearly suggests, in consequence, is that interpreters of the problem of women in Hawthorne can make a less autonomous use of Margaret Fuller than they have often supposed.)

To this point, as I have indicated, Hawthorne seems open to the charge of a fairly radical sort of reductivism: he seems to have presented an historical woman whose heretical ideas once caused a profound religious and social crisis as a simple case of uneasy or misplaced sexuality; and the opportunity to reduce Hester Prynne to a woman whose sexuality got quite literally out of control and never did entirely recover itself is therefore ready to hand. Such a reduction is, presumably, as distasteful to old male literary critics as it is to new women.

The way to stop being reductive and offensive about Hawthorne's use of the "female" Mrs. Hutchinson as a type of Hester Prynne is not, therefore, to appeal to the masterful modern psychohistorical interpretation of Mrs. Hutchinson's career. It is probably of some value to notice that its author (Emery Battis) devotes almost as many pages to the complicated female problems of her relation to her strong father, her weak husband, and her beloved pastor as he does to her ideas; that he convincingly urges a relation between menstrual cycle, pregnancy, menopause and the more public aspects of her career; and that he introduces his treatment of the character of this unusual woman with the astonishingly Hawthornian speculation that "had she been born into a later age, Mrs. Hutchinson might have crusaded for women's rights." It is perhaps more than a nice polemical point to observe that Hawthorne is not alone in reading sexual implications in Mrs. Hutchinson's theologic and prophetic career, but the observation leaves out all the subtle considerations. They concern not only the ways in which Ann Hutchinson and Hester Prynne are related in a very serious approach to the "theological" meaning of sexuality, but also the historical reasons Hawthorne had for linking enthusiasm, individualism, and femaleness.

If we glance again at the early sketch, we can notice that, embattled and argumentative as it is, it is yet about sex in some more elemental way than our discussion about "feminism" has so far indicated. With structural intention (and not, clearly, by obsession), the sketch tries hard to focus on several scenes in which Mrs. Hutchinson is the center of all male attention, prophesying doctrines that astound the male intellect. Most of the "historical" facts are there, but only a fairly well informed reader can feel assured of this; and except for an initial, one-paragraph reminder, the facts seem to fall out incidentally, so as not to distract from the dramatic confrontation. The implications, in turn, are not in the ordinary sense "theological": there is no mention of the famous eighty-two errors Mrs. Hutchinson is said to have spawned—as there is, self-consciously, in *Grandfather's Chair;* we are, historically and psychologically, beyond that sort of consideration. The issue is not sanctification as an evidence of justification, but the woman's own prophetic abilities. Having formerly cast aspersions on legal doctrines of salvation, the enthusiast now claims the spiritual "power of distinguishing between the chosen of man and the sealed of heaven." What further need of witnesses? Clearly the progress of the strange fire of her enthusiasm is far advanced.

Nor is there any significant ambiguity about the source and significance of that fire: Mrs. Hutchinson's spiritual openings and leadings are inseparable from her female sexuality. Although her "dark enthusiasm" has deceived the impetuous Vane and the learned but mildly illuministic Cotton, it is clearly her own "strange fire now laid upon the altar." The men, variously affected, must make of it whatever they can. Hawthorne does not quite identify enthusiasm with "the female," but we do not distort his intentions if—supplying our own italics—we take as the very heart of the sketch the following sentence: "In the midst, and in the center of all eyes, we see *the woman.*"

This may still be sexist, but it is no longer petty or carping. Mrs. Hutchinson's influence is indeed profound. Even the male chauvinist is compelled to admit it. The impulse to challenge the Puritan theocracy's dominant (and socially conservative) assumptions about "visible sanctity"evidently comes from a fairly deep and powerful source. It seems to be coming from—"the woman."

Evidently, in Hawthorne's view, fully awakened women accept the inevitability of a given legal order far less easily than their male counterparts. And clearly this is the central issue. What caused a state of near civil war in Boston and what creates the crackling tension in Hawthorne's sketch is Mrs. Hutchinson's proclamation—variously worded at various times, but always as far beyond the reach of the "trained and sharpened intellects" of the most scholastic Puritan controversialists as are Hester Prynne's sexual secrets—that "the chosen of man" are not necessarily "the sealed of heaven." Here, in her last, most devastating, and for Hawthorne most insupportable formulation, Mrs. Hutchinson is claiming that sort of direct inspiration and divine guidance necessary to distinguish between true and false, spiritual and legal teachers. But she has been forced to this last claim by the pressure of investigation and over-response; this, presumably, is what you are made bold to say when facing the legalistic integrity of John Winthrop—not to mention the holy wrath of Hugh Peters, the satiric antifeminism of Nathaniel Ward, and the sheer adamant intolerance of John Endicott. Behind her last claim—as Hawthorne well knows—lies a series of far less drastic attempts to affirm that the Spirit does not always obey the laws of ordinary moral appearance. And even though she has moved from the dangerous to the intolerable, the weight of Hawthorne's subtlest moral judgment falls no more heavily on her head than on those of her judges.

In simple ironic fact, she is their natural opposite—induced into individualistic heresy by their organized, legalistic intolerance in much the same way as Hester's later denials are induced by the violence of the community's over-response. Beginning, apparently, with only a purer sort of Calvinism than was customarily preached in New England, Mrs. Hutchinson's ultimate claim to a totally self-sufficient private illumination seems the inevitable response to an emerging Puritan orthodoxy which, in its undeniable tendency to conflate the visible with the invisible church, was really claiming that for nearly all valid human purposes the "chosen of men" *were* the "sealed of heaven." If the community overextends and mystifies its authority, the individual will trust the deepest passional self to nullify it all. Or at least "the woman" will.

What Hawthorne's figure of Mrs. Hutchinson suggests is that "the woman" is not by essence the safe and conserving social force the seventeenth and the nineteenth century (and much Hawthorne criticism) decreed her to be. On the contrary female sexuality seems, in its concentration and power, both a source for and a type of individualistic nullification of social restraint. Obviously Hawthorne's feelings about this are not without ambivalence. Personally, of course, he would always prefer some less powerful, more submissive "Phoebe"; and in one way or another he would continue to protest that "Woman's intellect should never give the tone to that of man," that her "morality is not exactly the material for masculine virtue." But his clear recognition of the antisocial meaning of self-conscious female sexuality, first formulated in the theological context of Puritan heresy, goes a long way toward explaining the power and the pathos of Hester Prynne.

Hawthorne reformulates his insight in "The Gentle Boy." Despite the complexities introduced by a "calm" male enthusiast and by the presence of the "rational piety" of that unreconstructed lover of home and children named Dorothy Pearson, we can hardly miss the elemental clash between "the female," Quaker Catherine, and the entire legalistic, repressive Puritan establishment. Against that male system of enforced rationalistic uniformity, she extravagantly testifies to the reality of an inspired and pluralistic freedom. Her response is, of course, extreme; Hawthorne is no more than faithful to history in judging it so (even though he does not have her walk naked through the streets of the Puritan capital). But, in a terrifying and elemental way, her response is effective. Tobias Pearson can only puzzle over and feel guilty about his drift toward the sect whose doctrines he thinks quite irresponsible; but this "muffled female" *must* stand up in the midst of a Puritan congregation (authoritatively and symbolically divided, by a wide aisle, into male and female) and denounce the minister's cruel and sterile formulation of the Puritan way.

The relevance of Quaker Catherine for Hester Prynne is simple and evident: here is the woman who has *not* been prevented from joining hands with Ann Hutchinson; her enthusiasm (and her sufferings) are such that not even little Ilbrahim can hold her back from a career of public testimony to the autonomous authority of conscience itself. Quaker Catherine does "come down to us *in history*, hand in hand with Ann Hutchinson." No doubt several historical women lie behind Hawthorne's figural portrait of Quaker Catherine, but surely none more powerfully than Mary Dyer, Ann Hutchinson's strongest female ally—who literally took her hand and accompanied her out of Cotton's church after her excommunication, went with her into exile, and (years after Mrs. Hutchinson had been providentially slaughtered by the Indians) went on to become notorious in the Quaker invasion of Massachusetts.

Accordingly, another level of history is also involved: virtually all commentators have recognized that in New England, in dialectic with the Puritan Way, Ann Hutchinson and the Quakers go together; that the latter represent, chiefly, a more organized and self-consciously sectarian espousal of the values of individualistic (or "spiritual") freedom which is the essence of Ann Hutchinson's doctrine. If one is committed and hostile, the cry against both is simply devilish and seductive enthusiasm, unregenerate impulse breaking all bonds of restraint and decorum. If one is committed and sympathetic, the cry is just as simple: the martyrdom of human dignity and divine freedom by aggressive repression. If one is a cautious modern commentator, one can only pity the victims and worry that both the Hutchinsonian and the (seventeenth-century) Quaker doctrines do rather tend to elevate the "individual conscience above all authority"; that both promote a "monistic egotism" which tends to dissolve "all those psychological distinctions man had invented to 'check, circumscribe, and surpass himself.' "

None of these formulations would have been unfamiliar to Hawthorne. And neither would his knowledge or speculation be significantly advanced by the modern historian who, after discussing the Ann Hutchinson question as a "Pre-Quaker Movement," begins his chapters on Quakerism proper with the observation that as in London and at the great Universities of England, "so too, the first Quakers to reach the American hemisphere were women" [Rufus Jones, *The Quakers in the American Colonies* (London, 1911)]. In every way it comes to seem the reverse of surprising that radical freedom and awakened female sexuality are inextricably linked in Hawthorne's most obviously historical romance. History itself had forged the link.

What is perhaps surprising is that Hawthorne is as sympathetic to a sex-related understanding of freedom as he is. His "Mrs. Hutchinson" is a profoundly troubled and dangerous woman; his Quaker Catherine becomes, in her "unbridled fanaticism," guilty of violating her most sacred duties (even if Ilbrahim is *not* a Christ-figure); even his Hester Prynne is far from the "Saint" she has occasionally been made out to be. But Hawthorne sympathizes with the problems as deeply as he fears the dangers; his compulsion to record warnings is no stronger than his desire to discover the laws by which powerful half truths generate their opposites or to feel the pain of those being destroyed by that implacable dialectic. The context of the sex–freedom link in *The Scarlet Letter* is not adequately sensed, therefore, until we are in a position to measure Hawthorne's emotional distance from his seventeenth-century sources who first raised the issue of sex in connection with Ann Hutchinson's law-denying theology.

The measurement is swiftly made. It begins with Cotton Mather and runs backward directly to John Winthrop and Edward Johnson. All three are, through the typology of Ann Hutchinson, important sources for *The Scarlet Letter*. And except that they are all highly scornful in tone, it might almost be said that these Puritan historians began the transformation of

Ann Hutchinson into Hester Prynne. Certainly they reduced Ann Hutchinson to a sexual phenomenon far more egregiously than did Hawthorne.

The emphasis of Cotton Mather's treatment of the Hutchinson controversy is double—but not very complex or subtle. On the one hand he utterly rejects the charge that his grandfather John Cotton was hypocritical in declining to espouse Ann Hutchinson as his partner in heresy: it is not, he pedantically insists, a case of a Montanus refusing to stand by the side of his Maxilla; rather, obviously, of a notorious woman whom an infamous calumny connected with the name of an Athanasius. (One thinks, perhaps, of certain obdurate refusals to believe Dimmesdale's final confession.) On the other hand, more expansively and with more literary flair, he is determined to treat the sectaries themselves in a frankly sexual way.

The following reflection—from a special sub-section titled "Dux Faemina Facta"—may stand for Mather's theological antifeminism:

> It is the *mark of seducers* that *they lead captive silly women*; but what will you say, when you hear *subtil women* becoming the most *remarkable* of the *seducers*? . . . Arius promoted his blasphemies by first proselyting seven hundred *virgins* thereunto. Indeed, a *poyson* does never insinuate so quickly, nor operate so strongly, as when *women's milk* is the *vehicle* wherein 'tis given. Whereas the prime seducer of the whole faction which now began to threaten the country with something like a Munster tragedy, was a woman, a gentlewoman, of "an haughty carriage, busie spirit, competent wit, and a voluble tongue."
>
> [*Magnalia Christi Americana*]

The quotation marks around the final descriptive phrase point back, of course, to a contemporary phase of antifeminist response to Ann Hutchinson. As usual Mather is only elaborating what has come down to him.

But equally important in the "Wonderbook" which so pervasively influenced Hawthorne is the primary sexual language which informs Mather's account. Far more memorable than any formulation concerning the self-evidence of justification is a bastardy metaphor which helped to shape *The Scarlet Letter*: the doctrines of the Antinomians are "brats" whose "true parents" are to be discovered by the guardians of orthodoxy. And related to this basic concept is the whole grotesque business of the "very surprising *prodigies*" which were looked upon as testimonies from heaven against the ways of the arch-heretic: "The erroneous gentlewoman herself, convicted of holding about *thirty* monstrous opinions, growing big with child . . . was delivered of about *thirty* monstrous births at once." Or—behold the

Puritan wit—perhaps "these were no more *monstrous births* than what is frequent for women, laboring with *false conceptions*, to produce."

Again, none of this is strictly original with Cotton Mather: the heretical-idea-as-illegitimate-child conceit is in the windy pages of Edward Johnson, and Winthrop himself labors the ugly details of monstrous births—which are at least the providential consequence of her criminal heresies. But the full "literary" elaboration of this sort of talk is Mather's, and his account seems most to have influenced Hawthorne.

The influence is very curious. On the one hand, Hawthorne specifically declines to repeat the story of monstrous births in his "Mrs. Hutchinson"; such details are fitter for the "old and homely narrative than for modern repetition." And the sketch makes no use of any bastardy metaphor. On the other hand, however, in a rather startling display of creative process, it all comes back in the story of Ann Hutchinson's typic sister, Hester Prynne. Not only does Hester conceive a very real, natural child to accompany (and in some measure embody) her quasi-Hutchinsonian conception of spiritual freedom; but she finds it almost impossible to convince herself that Pearl is not in some sense a monstrous birth. Along with many other characters in *The Scarlet Letter* (and not a few critics) Hester daily stares at the child, waiting "to detect some dark and wild peculiarity," unable to believe that a sinful conception can come to any valid issue. This *might* be no more than the too-simple Puritan inability ever to separate the moral order from the physical (like looking for "A's" in the midnight sky), but with Mather's elaboration of Johnson and Winthrop behind it, it is evidently a bit more. As almost everywhere, Hawthorne seems to be making Hester Prynne literally what orthodox Puritan metaphor said Ann Hutchinson was "really" or spiritually.

One more telling detail from Mather—to which we can only imagine Hawthorne's convoluted reaction. Not quite faithful to the wording of Winthrop, Mather has John Cotton express the opinion that Mrs. Hutchinson ought "to be cast out with them that 'love and make a lie.' "

Except for this peculiar formulation—which is not really related to Mather's basic set of sexual equivalences, but which just happens to read like an epitome of Dimmesdale's career—nearly all of Mather's basic vocabulary is second-hand. Mather's own debts are tedious to detail, and clearly Hawthorne could have got all he needed from the *Magnalia* (though it is certain he read most of Mather's sources independently). The basic antifeminist construction seems to originate with Winthrop—not only with his specific characterization of Mrs. Hutchinson as "a woman of a haughty and fierce carriage, of a nimble wit and active spirit, and a very voluble tongue" but also with the clear implication in his whole account that one very deep issue is Mrs. Hutchinson's female invasion of male "literary" prerogative. Mrs. Hutchinson insists, out of *Titus*, that "elder women should instruct the younger"; Winthrop might admit, under exegetical duress, that "elder women must instruct the younger about their business, and to love their husbands and not to make them to clash," but his deeper feeling is rationalized in *Timothy*: "I permit not a woman to teach."

This last makes the sexual politics of Hawthorne's remark about women's intellect not giving the tone to men's seem liberal. It also enables us to imagine, by simple contraries, what new and surer "relation between man and woman" Hester is teaching at the end of *The Scarlet Letter*. But, again, this is too easy.

If there is one formulation behind those of Cotton Mather worth savoring on its own, it is something from Edward Johnson. His impassioned account of the seductive appeal of Mrs. Hutchinson's doctrines gives us the clearest sense that Puritans themselves feared sexual implications more profound than those involving ordinary decorum. Upon Johnson's return to New England, he was alarmed to discover that a "Masterpiece of Woman's wit" had been set up by her own sex as a "Priest"; and Johnson was invited to join the cult:

> There was a little nimble tongued Woman among them, who said she could bring me acquainted with one of her own Sex that would shew me a way, if I could attaine it, even Revelations, full of such ravishing joy that I should never have cause to be sorry for sinne, so long as I live.
>
> [*Wonder-Working Providence of Sion's Saviour*]

Here, as clearly as we need, is the simply hostile version of Hawthorne's suggestion that "woman's morality is not quite the standard for masculine virtue"—as well as the perception, registered in anger and in fear, that antinomian doctrine is not separable from the tone and from the unsettling consequences of awakened female sexuality.

To write *The Scarlet Letter* out of Hutchinsonian materials Hawthorne would have to feel that tone, but he would have to feel others as well. Fear "the woman" as he might, he would yet feel the justice of setting her—in reality, and as a symbol of radical and self-contained moral freedom—against the omnivorous legalism of the Puritan establishment. If he would reduce Ann Hutchinson to a female "case," his reduction would be less drastic than that of his ancestors. And he would preserve, amplify, and revalue certain deeper hints. *The Scarlet Letter* might not be "about" Ann

Hutchinson, but it would be, consciously and emphatically, about anti-nomianism and "the woman."

II

We are now, finally, in a position to "begin"—to look directly at Hester walking in the footsteps of Ann Hutchinson, and to approach *The Scarlet Letter* itself in the one historical context Hawthorne seems most urgently to suggest. Legitimately, that task would require twice as many pages and distinctions as we have already set down. But perhaps the sympathetic reader will waive his right to charge reductive or text-ignoring historicism against a necessarily schematic suggestion about Hawthorne's romance in the Antinomian context.

The Scarlet Letter is, as I have suggested, not *roman à clef*: we are not to look for secret information about literal, existent singulars in the seventeenth-century world. Neither is it quite an "allegory" of the real significance of a theological controversy: the Antinomian Crisis has historical ramifications which defy critical ingenuity to discover in *The Scarlet Letter*. And yet, to repeat, it is about antinomianism and "the woman."

It is, as in one recent formulation, about "passion and authority," but it is not about those timeless human realities *as such*. The experiences of Hester and Dimmesdale are subject to an exquisite (and painful) historical conditioning. Their Puritan world may be, as in another formulation, some version of the "modern" world, but this is far too imprecise to account for the historical specificity of Hawthorne's intention and achievement. To be sure, *The Scarlet Letter* details the items of Hester's beliefs even less than the early sketch specifies those of Mrs. Hutchinson; and yet the romance undoubtedly is, as one very excellent reading describes it, a "literary exercise in moral theology."

That theology is, so far as the *characters* are concerned, "Puritan." So profoundly Puritan are the historically conditioned experiences of Hester and Dimmesdale, in fact, that *The Scarlet Letter* must be seen as Hawthorne's way of testing the limits of Puritan theology as a way of making sense out of the deepest and most passionate human experience. The limits of that theology are understood by Hawthorne to be—what I take it in fact they are—antinomian; and those antinomian limits of Puritan theology are associated by Hawthorne—as they were by his orthodox predecessors—with "the woman." When the limits are reached, as historically they were and as philosophically they must be, the theology fails what a twentieth-century critic of Puritanism has called "the pragmatic test." And as the theology fails, *The Scarlet Letter* becomes (in the context of the Ann Hutchinson problem, at least) a powerful contribution to what a nineteenth-century critic called "the moral argument against Calvinism."

The Scarlet Letter is about the reasons why "the woman" Hester Prynne reaches certain antinomian conclusions not unlike those of Ann Hutchinson; and why, though her progress seems somehow necessary, and though personally she enlists our deepest sympathies, both the tale and the teller force her to abandon those conclusions. More elliptically, it is also about Dimmesdale's lesser portion of the "strange fire"; about the failure of his Cottonesque, semi-antinomian theology; and, in the end, about his much-misunderstood "neonomian" emphasis on "the law" and "the sin." If we understand Hawthorne's relation to Mather, Johnson, and Winthrop properly, we can profitably view *The Scarlet Letter* as Hawthorne's own *Short Story of the Rise, Reign and Ruine of the Antinomians, Familists, and Libertines.*

In these terms, Hester's career is fairly easy to plot. At the outset she is not unambiguously antinomian. But she is conceived, like Hawthorne's Ann Hutchinson, as a woman who bears "trouble in her own bosom"; and her "desperate recklessness" on the scaffold, symbolized by the flagrancy of her embroidered "A," and issuing in a "haughty smile, and a glance that would not be abashed," seems deliberately to recall Mrs. Hutchinson's courtroom defiance:

> She stands loftily before her judges with a determined brow;
> and, unknown to herself, there is a flash of carnal pride half
> hidden in her eye, as she surveys the many learned and famous
> men whom her doctrines have put in fear.

That might describe Hester easily enough. She begins, let us say, in a not very repentant spirit. Strong hints of her later denials and unorthodox affirmations are already there.

To be sure, Hester feels a deep sense of shame, and we scarcely need the still, small quasi-authorial voice of a young woman spectator to tell us so; "the reduction" of Ann Hutchinson's doctrinal bastard to a living illegitimate child must, in a Puritan community, at least, count for something. And yet even here Hester feels little enough of what we should call "guilt." Just after the trauma of public exposure, she does confess a real wrong done to Chillingworth; but defiance of hopelessly unqualified and painfully uncomprehending male judges seems clearly the dominant element in her early characterization. It is probably true to say that (ignoring the "epilogue") Hester is nearer to "repentance" at the very opening of *The Scarlet Letter* than she ever is again. But she is not very near it. And by the time she finds herself in the forest with Dimmesdale, she has evidently found that she "should never have cause to be sorry for sinne" again.

For that antinomian moment, the narrator severely instructs us, Hester's "whole seven years of outlaw and ignominy had been little other than a preparation." The moment includes not only the decision to cast by all outward pretence of living by the Puritan "world's law" and run away with Dimmesdale but also, and even more radically, her attempt to convince that unreconstructed Puritan theologian that what they earlier did "had a consecration of its own"—they having felt it so and said so to each other. The painfulness of Hester's development toward this moment in no way lessens our sense of its inevitability. From the first she has seemed perilously close to defying her judges with the affirmation that her spirit posits and obeys its own law.

The narrator seems convinced that Hester has indeed sinned—deeply, and "in the most sacred quality of human life"; at one level of our response, the seventh commandment remains real enough. But what he urges far more strongly is the outrage to both human privacy and human conscience perpetrated by the enforced "unpardonable" Puritan practice of exposure and enforced confession. And he also feels—with Hester—that her adultery was, in quality, not entirely evil: the sacred is present along with the sinful; or, less paradoxically, that Hester has fulfilled her passionate self for the first time in her life.

But of course there are no Puritan categories for this ambiguity. There is no way for Hester to say to herself that her action had been naturally perfect and yet had introduced an element of profound social disharmony. And no way for the Puritan mind to treat her evident unwillingness *fully* to disown and un-will the affections and natural motions which caused the disorder as anything but evidence of unregenerate natural depravity. She evidently loves her sin, and theocrats in the business of inferring the ultimate moral quality of the self from the prevailing outward signs can reach only one conclusion. And, thus, when the Puritan establishment moves from the *fact* that Hester *has sinned* to the *conclusion* that she in essence *is sinful*, her rich and ambiguous personality has no life-saving resource but to begin a career of antinomian speculation, of internal resistance to all Puritan categories.

If Society must treat the negative implications of one mixed act as the symbol of the natural depravity of the Self, that Self is likely to respond with a simple affirmation of all its own profound impulses. If the Puritans begin by turning Hester into a sermon, a type, and an allegory of "Sin," she will end by nullifying their entire world of external law and interference with her own pure freedom. Ideally we might wish for Hester to cease feeling shame and to discover the real though limited extent of her guilt. But this, in the Puritan mental and social world, seems impossible. Extremes of public legalism seem to breed their antinomian opposite by natural law. At any rate, Hester finds no way to affirm the legitimacy of her powerful sexual nature without also affirming total, anarchic spiritual freedom.

Of course she begins in outward conformity, playing the game of "sanctification"—the single rule of which is that the true Self is the sum of all its outward works; indeed, by the time we see her in the chapter called "Another View of Hester," she has learned the game so well as to have covered her undestroyed inner pride with an external appearance "so like humility, that it produced all the softening influence of that latter quality on the public mind." But all the while she is "preparing," moving toward the moment when she announces a doctrine of personal freedom which every orthodox Puritan sensed would lead directly to passionate license and judged a more serious threat to public order than adultery itself.

Her own version of the antinomian heresy does not, obviously, express itself in theological jargon; for the most part Hawthorne eschewed it even in treating Mrs. Hutchinson. No dogmatist, Hawthorne is looking for differences that *make* a difference; and the antinomian difference is identically expressed in Mrs. Hutchinson and Hester Prynne, in association with but not quite reduced to a discovery and affirmation of the legitimacy of their female sexuality. Call it Spirit with the seventeenth, or Passional Self with a later century, one's affirmation is not very different: the significance of a life is *not* the sum of its legally regulated outward works; or, more radically, what one does has a consecration of its own provided the quality of deep inner feeling is right—i.e., authentic.

Now plainly this is all too partial a truth for Hawthorne; we are not wrong in hearing his own advice when Dimmesdale twice bids Hester's revolutionary voice to "Hush." And yet he understands how it all comes about. He even presents it as necessary for Hester to reach this stage of self-affirmation and release from shame before she can settle into anything approaching final peace.

While she cannot affirm her adultery, she cannot truly accept Pearl as a valid human person. It is probably too much to ask her to accept a good-out-of-evil doctrine all at once. Certainly it is better to affirm the natural order than to treat Pearl chiefly as a living sermon; clearly nothing good can happen as long as the mother is allegorizing the child even as the community has allegorized the mother; and surely a parent who is watching for a child to become a moral monster will not be disappointed.

And then there is the simple matter of Hester's integrity. Speculating so boldly and conforming so relentlessly, she has become—no less than Dimmesdale himself—two people. At one primal level, the whole antinomian controversy is about the inner and the outer, the private and the public person: what do our outward works, positive and negative, really reveal about our salvation status, or, in naturalized form, about our selves? Hawthorne's romance is, of course, busy denying total autonomous validity to the private or "spiritual" self; and the explicit "moral" about freely "showing forth" some inferential "token" clearly embodies the authorial realization that inner and outer can never be completely congruent. Hawthorne has not written "Young Goodman Brown" and "The Minister's Black Veil" for nothing. And yet Hester must stop living a life so completely double. Quite like Dimmesdale, she must heal the wide and deep, "hypocritical" split between her outer and inner self. She may never realize as clearly as Dimmesdale finally does the extent to which (or the profound reasons why) the Self must accept the demystified implications of the visible, and dwell—though not as the great body of Puritans do—among moral surfaces. But in the terms of her own developing theory of spiritual self-reliance, she must be, as fully as possible, whatever she truly is.

And we sense her self-acceptance and self-affirmation coming. She may seem to wander in confusion—thinking the sun of universal benevolence shines only to illuminate her scarlet letter, and deceiving herself about why she remains in New England; but from time to time, when a human eye (presumably Dimmesdale's) falls upon her "ignominious brand," she wills her old passion anew. She may worry about the condition and quality of Pearl's right to existence; but when the watchful theocratic government considers removing her natural child to some more socialized context of Christian nurture, Hester is simply defiant: "I will not lose the child!" She may argue from Pearl's moral use, but she is also affirming the validity of her sexual nature.

We can say—if we wish to maintain a *modern only* reading of *The Scarlet Letter*—that this is *all* Hester is affirming when she argues, finally, that her adultery had "a consecration of its own"; that Hawthorne has engaged Hester *entirely* in an *overt* struggle with the unruly and unsatisfied sexual emotions which the Puritans obscurely felt to lie unsublimated behind Mrs. Hutchinson's public career, and which they clearly felt would be unleashed upon their community by a public acceptance of her doctrine. (Male self-control being difficult enough when all women are passive or frigid.) But if our conclusions concern only Hester's movement from sexual shame to sexual affirmation, then Hawthorne has wasted a good deal of historic understanding and surmise as mere costume and color. It seems far more adequate to say—as we have already said—that Hawthorne regards awakened and not conventionally invested female sexual power as a source and type of individualistic nullification of social restraint.

Waiving the problem of vehicle and tenor, we may validly conclude that in *The Scarlet Letter* "the woman's" discovery of an authentic, valid, and not shameful sexual nature is not unlike the Self's discovery of its own interior, "spiritual" sanction. The *donnée* of Hawthorne's romance is such that Hester discovers both together, and each reinforces the other.

And further, by way of completing our contextual approach to *The Scarlet Letter*, it seems appropriate to suggest that Hawthorne's treatment of Dimmesdale, the less clearly antinomian partner, provides cogent reasons for not divorcing the theology from, or reducing it too simply to, sexuality. For Dimmesdale's predicament is not to be understood without some fairly explicit reference to the most theological of the antinomian questions—certainly not without a sense of the peculiar moral shapes one can be molded into only by a fairly high Calvinism. Indeed there is, as I have already suggested, strong evidence that Hawthorne thought of Dimmesdale as some intellectual and literary relative of John Cotton.

III

In a number of related senses, Dimmesdale's problem is "hypocrisy." Most simply, he is not what he outwardly appears; he may or may not be "vile," but he is not the apotheosis of saintly purity the Puritan community takes him for. More technically, he is an enforcing agent of public discipline who has himself sinned against a clear and serious public law whose absolute validity he (unlike Hester) never questions for a moment; and who refuses to confess and submit to the discipline he has sworn by covenant to uphold and enforce. In so refusing, he may very well be avoiding the question of whether he is really sorry for his sin, or whether in fact he loves his own satisfactions more than he loves God; if so, if Dimmesdale's adultery is really "idolatry," as in the common religious equivalence, then of course he is a "hypocrite" in the very most technical Puritan sense of all: he is an unconverted man who has found his way not only *in to* but to the very *apex* of the purest church the world has ever known. This is clearly what he fears: that the minister, whose election is sure if anyone's is, whose conversion is the norm for the members' admission, and who—at this level, incidentally—is universally revered as a miracle of preternatural holiness and supernatural humility, is really an unregenerate sinner simply.

He fears, but he is not certain. He also hopes. In such tension Dimmesdale is a classic Puritan case of conscience—an advanced and exacerbated form of the too-common problem of lingering sinfulness and naturally attendant doubt which seems to have followed most honest Puritans into full communion with New England's congregations of "visible saints." What, after all, could the unreconstructed Arminianism of natural conscience make of the fact that after one professed to have received saving grace by the direct operation of the spirit (and had that profession accepted by all other spiritual men) one continued to be roughly the same sort of moral person one was before?

The *simple* answer is antinomianism: "works" argue nothing. The sons of God being under no law, it is as fatal a confusion to argue from the presence of sin to the absence of grace as it is to infer justification of the person from sanctification of the life. Grace is a spiritual indwelling, and whatever the Spirit is, is right. Just ask Hester.

Dimmesdale, of course, can accept this limit-interpretation of Pauline and Protestant theology as little as Cotton could. And yet Dimmesdale seems caught in a trap set for him by certain of the spiritual principles Cotton laid down carefully to distinguish himself from both the covenant legalists on the one side and the "antinomians, familists, and libertines" on the other. Everyone wanted to admit that the forensic transaction of justification did not imply or create immediate and perfect operational sanctity, but Cotton's critics wanted him to narrow the gap as much as Protestant loyalty could possibly admit. They put it to him: when you say "A Christian may have assurance of his good estate maintained to him when the frame of his Spirit and course is grown much degenerate, we want much satisfaction." Your doctrine is very dangerous, they instructed him; there ought to be more "symmetry and proportion" in this matter of "faith and holiness" or you "open a wide door of temptation, as into Sin with less fear, so into a bold continuance and slight healing of sin, and breaches thereby."

As always, the legalists have conceived the problem rather too crudely: Dimmesdale's "continuance," for example, is far from "bold," and his physical and moral self-flagellations amount at some level to more than a "slight healing of sin." And yet there is sense in their position. A man who *fears* he may be a hypocrite and yet has good theological reasons to *hope* that even gross sins do not necessarily prove the case either way is likely to clutch at every available theological straw. And indeed Cotton's answer to the legalists offers far more than a straw. It is worth quoting at some length for it marvellously illuminates Dimmesdale's predicament. If a man

> know the riches of Gods grace in Christ, he ordinarily both may, and (by ordinary rule) ought to believe that his justified estate doth still remain unshaken, not withstanding his grievous sin. For as Justification and the faith of it doth not stand upon his good works, so neither doth it fall or fail upon his evil work.

Cotton's difference from the antinomians is, evidently, a fairly subtle one—and not of primary interest to us here. Of significance is the fact that the strictest Calvinist of New England's first generation provides Dimmesdale with a perfectly plausible way to avoid the obvious, most "natural" conclusion about his technical hypocrisy.

And Cotton brings the case even closer to our own:

> Because men of great measure of holiness be apt to live besides their faith, in the strength of their own gifts and not in the strength of Christ, it pleaseth the Lord sometimes to leave them to greater falls, than other weaker Christians, who being of weaker gifts do find more need to live by faith in Christ than upon the strength of their gifts.

It seems to me entirely likely that some conception such as this—a highly religious man being tested by a great fall—lies very close to Hawthorne's idea of Dimmesdale. And that Hawthorne is testing this Cottonesque way of conceptualizing the problem of sin and sainthood as he watches Dimmesdale fail to work out his salvation in these terms.

For the terms do fail him, even more plainly than, in the epilogue, Hester's appear to have failed her. The psychological dynamic of their failure is delicately wrought, but it is "there," in the romance. To see it requires only to look at Dimmesdale's few key speeches very closely.

We do not begin to get inside Dimmesdale until Chapter 10, where "The Leech" is working on "His Patient." With the worst imaginable motives, Chillingworth is trying to get Dimmesdale to do what the structure and basic conception of the romance clearly indicates he must if he is to save his soul, in any imaginable sense—clearly and openly admit his guilt, whatever the consequences. Dimmesdale offers several "good" reasons why some men find it impossible to confess before the Last Day, to any but the Searcher of Hearts. His reasons are all, we easily sense, speculative or notional, unreal; the two men are talking "objectively" about "some men." And yet before Dimmesdale waives the whole subject as if "irrelevant or unreasonable," he is betrayed into a modestly revealing hint. The best of his rationalizations is that "some men" do not confess because in spite of their sin they yet retain "a zeal for God's glory and man's welfare"; they realize that once exposed "no good can be achieved by them; no evil of the past be redeemed by better service." Hypocrisy, Dimmesdale seems to argue, is not without an important social, even spiritual use.

Chillingworth, however, that perfect devil's advocate, recognizes the desperate character of this logic at once. Hypocrisy for the sake of the kingdom is the worst hypocrisy of all. Would Dimmesdale have us believe "that a false show can be better—can be more for God's glory, or man's welfare—than God's own truth"?

The irony here is very keen. It seems impossible to escape the sense that Hawthorne is deliberately playing with one of the most famous arguments in a massive Puritan literature of propagandistic self-defense—the idea of "the usefulness of hypocrites." Attacked by English Presbyterians for a wildly utopian collapse of the invisible church into the visible, defenders of the New England Way loudly protested that they fully *expected* to receive hypocrites into their churches, despite the revolutionary tests for saving grace; that they indeed could rest easy in this practical knowledge, despite their purist theoretic aims, because in outward practice the hypocrite was very often more zealous, set a more striking public example than the true saint. The most authoritative spokesman for this Puritan "foreign policy" was—of course—John Cotton.

The irony is only slightly less telling when we remember that neither Dimmesdale nor Hawthorne really sees the case in these terms. Hawthorne could very *easily* accept hypocrites into *his* church, since it is universal and consists *only* of hypocrites who never *can* fully "show forth" what they ultimately are. Limited to his historic world, however, Dimmesdale is obviously far from this insight. Indeed he is even farther away from it than his use-of-hypocrites rationalization would indicate.

Where he is, morally and theologically speaking, becomes perfectly clear only in the forest with Hester—though anyone versed in the literary cure of Puritan souls senses it long before. The meaning of his entire predicament is encapsulated into two sentences, and logically enough he speaks them in direct reply to Hester's antinomian plan for adulterous escape:

> "If, in all these past seven years," thought he, "I could recall one instant of peace or hope, I would yet endure, for the sake of that earnest of Heaven's mercy. But now,—since I am irrevocably doomed,—wherefore should I not snatch the solace allowed to the condemned culprit before his execution?"

Again the irony is fairly complex. First of all we recognize in Dimmesdale's decision to "seize the day" the crassest sort of antinomian response possible for a Calvinist to make: since I am predestined to hell anyway, I might as well. . . . But this is the least of it.

More crucially, Dimmesdale reveals that he has to this point been looking at his life in a way that is very "properly" Calvinist: he has been regarding his acts, good and evil, and his spiritual states, hopeful and discouraging, not as sequential parts of a moral life that he is *building*, bit by bit, but rather as *evidences* of his status relative to divine decree. The difference may often seem subtle in practice, but it is absolutely profound; and the meaning is to be read in any Puritan diary. One does not repent sin in order to undo it and atone for it and get back into divine favor; only Catholics and other Arminians think this. Rather one examines sins along with every other significant fact about the moral life in order to detect, if one possibly can, whether or not an eternal decree of salvation has made itself temporally manifest as a spiritual experience of justification, usually issuing more or less "proportionally and symmetrically" in sanctification.

For *most* Puritans sins are, therefore, an essential sign; for *all*, repentance is an absolutely necessary one. Even for Cotton. The great man may have great sins and not lose heart and hope; but even the great man must find that he truly *can* repent. Gross outward lapses may be at best a crude indicator of the spiritual estate, but enduring love of sin is not.

"Of penance," Dimmesdale admits—of that melodramatic outward punishment and gothic inward torture—there has been a surfeit; "Of penitence," however—of that true spiritual rejection of the soul's rejection of God—"there has been none!" And now, he concludes, things look very bad indeed. He may as well admit he has been, all along, the hypocrite he feared he might be and yet hoped (in spite of his rationalization to Chillingworth) he might not be. In the forest then, finally, after seven years of self-torturing hope against hope, Dimmesdale gives over the attempt to see himself as the man whose justification does not, in Cotton's words, "Fall or fail upon his evil works." Semi-antinomian to this point, he now concludes that his hope has all been in vain—that he has not repented his sin, that he has been granted no further spiritual assurances, and that his crime of adultery is precisely what all vulgar Puritanism would take it to be, "visible" (if only to himself) evidence of manifest unregeneracy.

Spiritually, then, Dimmesdale is further from Hester Prynne during their sexual reunion in the forest than he has ever been before—as far away, in fact, as it is possible to be within a Puritan world. Their decision to escape, though they may "say it" to each other, means two dramatically opposed things. To Hester it is that triumphant escape into the higher antinomian freedom of spiritual self-reliance; to Dimmesdale it is a pitiful retreat from the hope-against-hope to that miserable alternative of sinful freedom left to the despairing reprobate. One may wish their original adulterous meeting involved more of real mutuality.

Thus Hawthorne's subtlest view of Dimmesdale is as a man who is so ineffectual an antinomian as not to be able to overcome the conscientious suspicion that his serious sin proves him a hypocrite; not even with the subtle categories of John Cotton. Hawthorne's men, as we know, are weaker than his women. Or perhaps it is simply that "woman's morality is not quite the standard for masculine virtue." Or perhaps he is simply honest. In any event, neither his sexuality nor his doctrine can justify the life he has been leading or, now, sanctify the new freedom he has been seduced into accepting. He will run away, in a sense, to settle his doubts, once and for all, into a certainty of reprobation.

If we are sufficiently aware of the positivistic pitfalls, it becomes useful to speculate about Dimmesdale's fictional relation to John Cotton. Should we say he is some curious version of Cotton's son, who did commit adultery and suffer ignominious excommunication? Or might we see him as a provisional John Cotton who by Providential mischance happened to seduce (or be seduced by) Ann Hutchinson? What if, Hawthorne might have brooded, what if Ann Hutchinson had literally been what Puritan metaphor implied she was? And what if Cotton were implicated, literally, to the very extent his English detractors said he metaphorically was? What, in short, would a "high" but not antinomian Calvinist do if he *had* played the part of a sexual Montanus to some sexual Maxilla? What would a real sin, all passionate and ambiguous, do to the delicate balances of personality required to maintain that exquisite "Doctrine of the Saints' Infirmities"? What sense might a younger, less robust, less settled version (or disciple) of Cotton be able to make out of a passionate adultery?

In this light, it is just possible that Dimmesdale owes something to the writings (*not* to the *life*) of John Preston, Cotton's most famous orthodox convert and disciple. Mather's *Magnalia* calls Cotton the "spiritual father" of Preston, and his most famous work (*The Doctrine of the Saints' Infirmities*, 1638) owes a profound debt to Cotton's ideas about assurance in spite of sin. Like Cotton, Preston is at great pains to prove that the Puritan saint "may have many infirmities, and the covenant remain unbroken." But there is one peculiar and illuminating hesitation in Preston that is entirely lacking in Cotton's answers to the American legalists of the 1630s. Unlike Cotton, Preston is anxious about an exception—or at least a possible misunderstanding. Not *all* sins can be written off as mere "infirmities"; "some sins" are so radically idolatrous that they must be taken to mean that a person has not *been* in the covenant—that he has been a hypocrite all along. Preston does not specify; but his one hint is telling indeed: the exceptions are sins which "untye the marriage knot" as, in human marriage, "Adultery." That revelation would seem to explain Dimmesdale's career pretty well: the reason he *cannot* repent is that he *is not* a saint; *probably* Preston's emphasis is sounder than Cotton's. And so he gives over the desperate seven-year effort to believe himself *not* a hypocrite in the worst sense. His peculiar "infirmity" is too real, too true a sign of unregenerate infidelity. Justification and sanctification are not to be conflated, but "some sins" are unsupportable. And thus, until Dimmesdale's very last moment, Puritan doctrines with sexual implications and overtones seem to be damning him as surely as they seem to be saving Hester.

At the last moment, of course, a major reversal occurs. Ceasing to "live in the strength of [his] own gifts"—even though he has just exercised them magnificently in a bad-faith election sermon—Dimmesdale asks for Hester's strength and God's grace to help him up the scaffold. Once there, his words indicate that somehow he has freed himself from his old Calvinist entrapment. If he has not entirely de-theologized himself, at least he has got his doctrine down to certain saving essentials. Hester calls on his far-seeing vision to predict their final destiny. But Dimmesdale, who has been reading evidences of *faits accomplis* for too long, rightly refuses to predict: "Hush, Hester, hush!" What has often been called his final "gloom" is no more than elemental moral and theological honesty. "The law we broke!—the sin here so awfully revealed!" Stern instructions to an antinomian. Yet these alone must be in their thoughts, their only proper concern. For the rest, "God knows; and He is merciful!"

Law, Sin, Mercy—these are now the only terms in Dimmesdale's new moral scheme. We know there are laws to restrict our Selves in the name of our communities which, well or ill, sustain our common life; we know we break these laws; the rest is up to God. This may or may not conceal Arminian heresy, but "neonomian" Hawthorne has clearly designed it to be. I think we may grant the writer of "Young Goodman Brown" and "The Minister's Black Veil," and the creator of Dimmesdale's problems of ever "outering" what he truly is inside, the right to affirm the operational primacy of "the public."

It takes Hester longer, and it requires a years-later epilogue, but she too relents from her doctrine of the autonomous private—she repents, turns her game of "penance" into authentic "penitence." She still holds out for a feminist reformer, but she can now separate the valid sexual expectations of her sisterhood from the supposed spiritual freedom of the Self from the world's law.

The final ironies of Hawthorne's use of Hutchinsonian motifs and antinomian ideas are striking indeed. If his early sketch seems to reduce a dangerous female heretic to a sexual case, his effort can be regarded as a commentary on a Puritan response as validly as it can be taken for his own; and, he puts *all* the subtlety back into *The Scarlet Letter*. He maintains, even literalizes, all the sexual suggestions in his creation of Hester Prynne, but he leaves them in tension with some very profound (if, for him, dangerous) religious ideas. With Dimmesdale he allows the full theological complexity to operate, though we never forget that Dimmesdale is related to Hester in the sexual problems which form the context of their spiritual struggles. The perfect context, we feel, given Puritan problems with "privacy" of all sorts. And in the end, after he has fully explored the antinomian and Cottonesque ramifications of his imaginative vision of a Puritan heresy, in doctrine and in metaphoric implication, Hawthorne brings both his principal characters back to something like his own "neonomian" norm. The ending is by no means "happy"—any more than Hawthorne's "Antinomians" and "Libertines" are in any sense that would satisfy Winthrop or Mather "Ruined." But their "Short Story" does end in an important doctrinal transformation.

The Self is not to be regularly inferred from its Works; it is quite naive to think so. But human sin, guilt, and sorrow are not to be transcended or "spiritually" suspended in this life. The Self is spiritually more free than any human establishment, theocratic or otherwise, can recognize or "tolerate." But the world's law validly exists to restrain our disruptive social excesses, however powerful and authentic we feel or "say" their private consecration to be. That, or something like it, equally simple, was the usable historical truth to be discovered from a tracing of Ann Hutchinson's footsteps.

Hawthorne by Moonlight

Richard H. Brodhead

> Whatever may have been Hawthorne's private lot, he has the
> importance of being the most beautiful and most eminent rep-
> resentative of a literature. . . . He is the writer to whom his
> countrymen most confidently point when they wish to make a
> claim to have enriched the mother-tongue, and, judging from
> present appearances, he will long occupy this honourable
> position.

Henry James's claim for the value of his subject at the opening of his critical
essay *Hawthorne* is interesting in that he presents it not as a personal opinion
but as an authoritative statement of a self-evident truth. As such these lines
reflect a curious feature of the history of Hawthorne's reputation. If there
is some justice to Hawthorne's own claim to have been for many years the
obscurest man of letters in America, it is remarkable how quickly and how
generally he came to be seen, starting about the time he was publishing his
major novels, as one of the most illustrious—as a writer whose achievement
was of such an order as to offer a shining example of what an American
author could do. Hawthorne no longer stands quite so alone as an eminent
case as he did for James, but he retains a special place in the tradition of
American fiction as a master and originator. However interesting the works
of Cooper and Poe may be, *The Scarlet Letter* is the first genuine masterpiece
among American novels, and it is as well the first American novel that

From *Hawthorne, Melville, and the Novel.* © 1973, 1976 by The University of Chicago. The University of Chicago Press, 1976.

other novelists have continued to regard as suggesting possibilities for their own art. The admiration of figures like Melville, James, Howells, and Faulkner, as well as George Eliot and D. H. Lawrence, is a finer tribute than that of popular reputation, for it is the tribute of fellow artists to the power of Hawthorne's vision and to his command of their common craft.

In view of Hawthorne's stature as a novelist it always comes as something of a surprise to recall that writing novels was a belated second career for him. After the abortive *Fanshawe* he confined himself to the shorter forms of fiction for twenty years. And his eventual turn to the novel was not, really, the result of his work's accumulated momentum. As he himself recognized, the direction of his most mature work is better indicated by his earliest tales than by the sketches of the 1840s. Certainly it is his whole literary achievement, and not just his novels, that qualifies him for James's "honourable position." But Hawthorne tended to consider story-writing and novel-writing as separate endeavors in his artistic life. His attitude toward his shorter works is a complex one, worth considering for a moment for the light it sheds on the crucial transition in his career.

If we can translate his word in the prefaces to *Twice-Told Tales* and *Mosses from an Old Manse*, what strikes Hawthorne as he reviews the accumulated production of two decades is its perpetual failure to amount to anything worthwhile. He presents these collections to us as bedraggled and faded bouquets. His twice-told tales have, to him, "the pale tint of flowers that blossomed in too retired a shade"; the new pieces in *Mosses* are "idle weeds and withering blossoms," while the older ones are "faded things, reminding me of flowers pressed between the leaves of a book." This note of self-deprecation is, of course, characteristic of all Hawthorne's public presentations of himself, and it is not always to be taken at face value. But his evaluations of his short works are cast in terms of imaginative patterns of such urgency in his thought that they must be taken seriously, if not literally. When he sees his ancestors scoffing at his career in "The Custom-House"—" 'A writer of storybooks! What kind of business in life, —what mode of glorifying God, or being serviceable to mankind in his day and generation,—may that be?' "—Hawthorne has no ready answer with which to meet them, and his problem is made all the harder by his own partial allegiance to the standard they invoke against him, his own belief in the value of sharing in "the united effort of mankind." When he writes that the pictures of life in *Twice-Told Tales* are "not always so warmly dressed in its habiliments of flesh and blood, as to be taken into the reader's mind without a shiver," and when he calls the contents of *Mosses* "fitful sketches, with so little of external life about them, yet claiming no profundity of purpose," he links his work to the chill shadow worlds, devoid of human warmth and reality, that stand as a peculiarly horrible sort of death-in-life all through his fiction.

Hawthorne shows the position of the creator of such airy nothings in "The Devil in Manuscript." "By aping the realities of life" Oberon succeeds only in emptying that life of its reality and "surrounding myself with shadows." And his preoccupation with his imagined creatures leads him "into a strange sort of solitude — a solitude in the midst of men—where nobody wishes for what I do, nor thinks nor feels as I do." Not only is he not serviceable to mankind; his art has severed him from sustaining contact with the vital chain of human concern. Obviously Hawthorne's position as an author is not simply identical to Oberon's. But his insistence in each preface that "I have done enough in this kind" indicates an abiding discontent with his shorter works, and to the extent that his deprecations of them are sincere they are based on a revulsion from the sense of unreality and isolation of which "The Devil in Manuscript" presents the extreme instance.

Hawthorne records a particularly interesting fit of this revulsion in "The Old Manse." As he approaches his new home in Concord, the manse's former occupants, its eight generations of saintly divines, seem almost physically present to him. The sense of the holy and strenuously thoughtful work to which this spot is consecrated has the effect of making its first lay inhabitant pause to reconsider the direction of his own career. The first stage of this reassessment is simply negative. In the presence of the manse's spirit of high seriousness "I took shame to myself for having been so long a writer of idle stories." But he immediately discovers that the spirit of this place also enables him to form more positive conceptions of new vocational possibilities. Completely yielding his own claims and imagining an identity for himself in terms of the strong tradition of the place, he sees that he might write books in the divines' own vein, "profound treatises of morality." Or—and here he gradually begins to distance himself from the divines—he might retain their matter but treat it from his own more secular point of view, writing "a layman's unprofessional, and therefore unprejudiced views of religion." Or he might transfer their habit of serious meditation to a secular subject matter and produce "histories . . . bright with picture, gleaming over a depth of philosophic thought." And finally: "I resolved at least to achieve a novel, that should evolve some deep lesson, and should possess physical substance enough to stand alone."

At this critical juncture Hawthorne works his way through the manse's forcefully presented ideal to a point at which the role of artist once more seems valid to him. What enables him to come full circle in this way is his ability to conceive of a new form for his art. To win his own self-approval here he needs to feel that he too is capable of undertaking a large and serious treatment of the nature of human existence; and he locates the capacity for this sort of treatment in the novel. As a novelist he will be dealing with physical substance, not shadows; as he evolves deep lessons he will be able to claim a profundity of purpose; if he will not be directly engaged in the united struggle of mankind, his solitude will now have the character not of sterile isolation but rather of the "accessible seclusion" of the divines themselves, who step apart from the everyday life of humanity only to the end of serving as its source of self-comprehension. By rejecting the idle story and embracing the novel he will be changing not just the genre but the whole nature and value of his art. And although the novels he was later to write are not quite of the kind that he envisions in his last resolution, Hawthorne's gravitation toward the larger genres of fiction must be understood as a function of the commitment to an earnest imaginative address to human experience that he dramatizes here.

Hawthorne did not carry out his resolution at the Old Manse. To observe his actual emergence as a novelist we must turn from "The Old Manse" to the next chapter of his spiritual autobiography, "The Custom-House." In accepting the position of Salem's customs inspector Hawthorne seems to have found a more efficient way of releasing himself from the prison of mental solitude and joining in the real life of men. Reacting against the excessive imaginativeness and intellectuality of Concord life he welcomes his new duties as a chance for him to "exercise other faculties of my nature, and nourish myself with food for which I had hitherto had little appetite." But he quickly sees that his apparent involvement with actual experience here is delusory; this existence threatens to become even more inauthentic than his previous one. As he contemplates the enervating effect that public life has had on the officers of the Custom-House he comes to wonder whether the private imaginative resources he had been content to let lie suspended may not be in danger of permanent destruction.

The central action of "The Custom-House" shows how Hawthorne enters into this "unnatural state" and how he gains release from it. The essay's movement repeats his own: it begins outside the Custom-House and slowly moves up to and into the building, until finally, in its innermost corner, Hawthorne makes a discovery that brings about a rebirth of his imaginative powers, a discovery that permits him to come forth from the building and his false life there—and to come forth a novelist. "The

Custom-House" purports to prove the authenticity of the materials of *The Scarlet Letter*, but what it actually testifies to is the authenticity of the creative energy of *The Scarlet Letter*'s author. Its climactic episode shows how the scarlet letter that Hawthorne finds, like the lady in "Drowne's Wooden Image," "first created the artist who afterwards created her image."

Hawthorne's account of the discovery of the scarlet letter is extremely deliberate in its pace. We are told how he found the bundle of old documents in an upper room, how he recalled the history of Surveyor Pue, and then how he came upon "a certain affair of fine red cloth, much worn and faded." The discovery of materials goes along with a slow kindling of interest. At first Hawthorne notes that he is affected with pleasure; then a chance discovery "quickened an instinctive curiosity"; and finally he finds his attention "most drawn" by the letter. Even after he is thus drawn to it the process of perception continues slowly, step by step: he examines its needlework; then he perceives that the rag is a letter; he measures its sides; he makes surmises about its possible uses as an article of apparel. But in the midst of this investigation he is seized by the letter, fascinated, held fast; the slow process of discovery quickens to a climactic response.

> My eyes fastened themselves upon the old scarlet letter, and would not be turned aside. Certainly, there was some deep meaning in it, most worthy of interpretation, and which, as it were, streamed forth from the mystic symbol, subtly communicating itself to my sensibilities, but evading the analysis of my mind.

And this climax, rather than terminating Hawthorne's discovery, ensures that it will continue. Having engaged the letter with his understanding, and having then felt it engaging his sensibilities, he now comes—again by an accident which is almost like fate—to yet another kind of knowledge and response, this time a physical one: holding the letter to his chest while he muses, he feels it exuding a burning heat.

At this point the tone of excitement modulates, first into a more matter-of-fact one, as Hawthorne tells of finding "a small roll of dingy paper . . . containing many particulars respecting the life and conversation of one Hester Prynne," and then into a rather comic one, as Hawthorne gives his pseudo-gothic account of meeting Surveyor Pue's ghost. In this meeting, having been in effect chosen by the symbol, he accepts the responsibility of telling its story. The surviving past that has reawakened his own powers of imagination now requires from him a commitment to the task of imagi-

natively reconstructing that past. Pue comes to him as his "official ancestor," but the office that this encounter forces him to undertake is that of
an inspector of customs with a difference; he is to become simultaneously
a student of antiquities and an inventor of fictions.

Hawthorne's celebrated description of the moonlit room provides the
one crucial account in his works of how his vision becomes transformed
into fiction. The passage has a logic and a rhythm of its own, so that it
must be cited in full.

> The same torpor, as regarded the capacity for intellectual effort,
> accompanied me home, and weighed upon me in the chamber
> which I most absurdly termed my study. Nor did it quit me,
> when, late at night, I sat in the deserted parlour, lighted only
> by the glimmering coal-fire and the moon, striving to picture
> forth imaginary scenes, which, the next day, might flow out on
> the brightening page in many-hued description.
>
> If the imaginative faculty refused to act at such an hour, it
> might well be deemed a hopeless case. Moonlight, in a familiar
> room, falling so white upon the carpet, and showing all its
> figures so distinctly—making every object so minutely visible,
> yet so unlike a morning or noontide visibility—is a medium the
> most suitable for a romance-writer to get acquainted with his
> illusive guests. There is the little domestic scenery of the well-
> known apartment; the chairs, with each its separate individuality;
> the centre-table, sustaining a work-basket, a volume or two,
> and an extinguished lamp; the sofa; the book-case; the picture
> on the wall;—all these details, so completely seen, are so spiri-
> tualized by the unusual light, that they seem to lose their actual
> substance, and become things of intellect. Nothing is too small
> or too trifling to undergo this change, and acquire dignity
> thereby. A child's shoe; the doll, seated in her little wicker car-
> riage; the hobby-horse;—whatever, in a word, has been used or
> played with, during the day, is now invested with a quality of
> strangeness and remoteness, though still almost as vividly pres-
> ent as by daylight. Thus, therefore, the floor of our familiar
> room has become a neutral territory, somewhere between the
> real world and fairy-land, where the Actual and the Imaginary
> may meet, and each imbue itself with the nature of the other.
> Ghosts might enter here, without affrighting us. It would be
> too much in keeping with the scene to excite surprise, were we

to look about us and discover a form, beloved, but gone hence, now sitting quietly in a streak of this magic moonshine, with an aspect that would make us doubt whether it had returned from afar, or had never once stirred from our fireside.

The somewhat dim coal-fire has an essential influence in producing the effect which I would describe. It throws its unobtrusive tinge throughout the room, with a faint ruddiness upon the walls and ceiling, and a reflected gleam from the polish of the furniture. This warmer light mingles itself with the cold spirituality of the moonbeams, and communicates, as it were, a heart and sensibilities of human tenderness to the forms which fancy summons up. It converts them from snow-images into men and women. Glancing at the looking-glass, we behold—deep within its haunted verge—the smouldering glow of the half-extinguished anthracite, the white moonbeams on the floor, and a repetition of all the gleam and shadow of the picture, with one remove farther from the actual, and nearer to the imaginative. Then, at such an hour, and with this scene before him, if a man, sitting all alone, cannot dream strange things, and make them look like truth, he need never try to write romances.

In the moonlit parlor nature meets imagination halfway. The moonlight illumines the individual outlines of things but at the same time breaks down the boundaries between thing and thought, transforming everything into "things of intellect." It functions therefore as an analogy for the imagination; and, by thus setting a good example, it also functions as a stimulus to the imagination. When he observes the moonlight spiritualizing the furniture, Hawthorne's mind begins to realize its own creatures. The natural process of moonlight initiates an imaginative process that works in exactly the opposite direction, giving actuality and substance to things of intellect, but in such a way that the two can seem to meet and mingle before the author in a vivid interaction pattern.

This passage has such a brilliant metaphorical vitality that it is easy to lose sight of its immediate occasion. Hawthorne goes to the parlor and cultivates the experience of magic moonshine there in response to his specific needs and difficulties as a creator of fiction. After he discovers the scarlet letter, the continuing routine of his official life makes his imagination "a tarnished mirror" that "would not reflect, or only with miserable dimness, the figures with which I did my best to people it." He resorts to the natural magic of the moonlit room in an effort to liberate his creative fancy. He wants to get acquainted with his "illusive guests," to make them available to him as characters for his fiction; he wants to "picture forth imaginary scenes" which, when written out the next day, will compose his fiction's action and plot.

Hawthorne's problem is not just that his imagination is torpid; it is that the kind of imaginative energy the symbol ignited in him does not, at this stage, lend itself to fictional creation. The letter overwhelms him with an epiphanic revelation, communicating an impression of total meaningfulness to his sensibilities but refusing to yield up its meaning to his analytical understanding. The symbol's communication is instantaneous; it has nothing to do with the sort of sequential experience that a narrative could be composed of. As Hawthorne's eyes fasten themselves on the letter the tremendous meaning that streams forth from it is not even a human meaning. And the ingredients for a story, the potential characters and actions outlined in the roll of dingy paper, are at this point separate from his source of inspiration.

The symbol burns Hawthorne with its heat, but "the characters of the narrative would not be warmed and rendered malleable, by any heat that I could kindle at my intellectual forge." In the terms of this metaphor Hawthorne's task in the moonlit room is to get the symbol to animate his characters with its warm life. To do so he induces in himself a reverie state like that described in "The Haunted Mind," a state in which

> the mind has a passive sensibility, but no active strength; when the imagination is a mirror, imparting vividness to all ideas, without the power of selecting or controlling them. . . . You sink down in a flowery spot, on the borders of sleep and wakefulness, while your thoughts rise before you in pictures.

In his reverie he relinquishes his powers of selection and control, and he relinquishes the kind of sense that his conscious mind can make of his corpselike characters, in order to have them come before him on their own terms as the creatures of his fantasy. He allows them to present to him his own thoughts, the processes of his own buried mind, dramatically and pictorially. In this way the part of his mind that communed with the mystic symbol can come before him in the form of a potential narrative. The symbol's deep meaning is metamorphosed into characters and their action. And by analyzing the "motives and modes of passion" of these characters later on he can thus make articulate and comprehensible the meaning that in the first place evaded "the analysis of my mind." Of all the things that meet and mingle in the moonlit room the crucial coalescence for the author is that of symbol and story; in its light we can understand Hawthorne's whole experience in the room as a kind of rite by which he courts the muse of narrative fiction.

Hawthorne's account of the discovery of the scarlet letter is itself an invention, but as a presentation of his process of inspiration this account seems accurate enough. "Endicott and the Red Cross" and an entry in his *American Notebooks* demonstrate that Hawthorne was fascinated by the scarlet letter as a symbol long before he attempted to work out its implications in the form of a dramatic tale. And "The Custom-House" also seems accurate in its suggestion of the place of narrative in Hawthorne's process of creation. Its pattern can be detected over and over in his works. As he leads his readers down to the monument to the Battle of Concord in "The Old Manse" he tells of how he heard about the boy who killed the wounded British soldier with his ax, and then he adds, "the story comes home to me like truth." His own response, like his response to the letter, transcends the linear and specifically human dimensions of the story. Then, to get at the "truth" that comes home to him, he has to go on to imagine more of the story; he undertakes "as an intellectual and moral exercise" to envision the rest of the boy's life. The germ of "Wakefield" is a remembered report of a strange episode of marital dereliction that fills Hawthorne with "wonder, but with a sense that the story must be true." And again, to discover the content of this felt revelation, he proceeds to invent a narrative action. For Hawthorne creation characteristically begins with an arresting response, an encounter in which his whole mind gathers to receive an intimation of inarticulate truth. To make these truths comprehensible he must reverse his mind's initial centripetal motion and, by resorting to conventions of character, scene, and plot, translate them into an image of unfolding human experience.

Telling a story is in this way necessary for Hawthorne; it is only through his narrative embodiment that he can unpack the truths that come home to him. But is should also be noted that Hawthorne does not begin with plot and character, and that even as he gives himself to the task of imagining his characters' lives he retains an interest in exploring, through them, a "deep meaning" that is of a different order from the experiential one. Because of this there is always a potential gap in his fiction between the meaning that is his characters' experience and the meaning that their experience can be seen as symbolizing. Hawthorne is an intensely dramatic novelist without ever becoming a completely dramatic novelist; and the tendency of his work to include structures of meaning somewhat distinct from that of their human interactions can be understood as the product of this initial doubleness within his creative process.

As a model for the operation of the imagination Hawthorne's moonlit room suggests the basis for another tension within his fictional forms as well. In the room the moon, by making the actual seem strange and spiritual, encourages the author to project his ghostly guests before him, and the red tinge of the coal fire then makes these guests seem warm and substantial. The room's lighting makes discontinuous orders of reality seem continuous, so that the mirror can repeat back the whole scene without marking differences between the imaginary and the actual. By analogy the author is able to imagine scenes which he can write out the next day because in this haunted place images of actuality become malleable to him, capable of imaginative reordering, and at the same time the figures of his reverie seem to become human and to live out actual lives. And, like the mirror, his mind can receive back the mixed world he has created as if it were uniformly real and as if it existed independent of him.

Because the presence of so many of Hawthorne's own favorite images gives this passage a highly personal cast, it is necessary to stress the fact that the imaginative activity he is describing is not his and his alone. In a discussion of Balzac, Albert Béguin writes:

> A fictional society, when it is the work of a great artist, arises at the point where two different projections meet: the projection into the imaginary of a real world which the novelist has recorded to the best of his ability; and the projection into reality of a personal myth, expressing his self-knowledge, his knowledge of fate, his notion of the material and spiritual forces whose field is the human being.

Béguin's terms and emphases are obviously not as well suited to Hawthorne's work as they are to Balzac's, but in their comprehensiveness his comments help to show the more general implication of what goes on in the moonlit room. Clearly Béguin's system of double projections is exactly analogous to what Hawthorne describes; his point where two projections meet is Hawthorne's neutral territory. The novelist creates that territory for himself when he is capable of giving his imagination's order to the actual as its logic and of giving the actual's texture to his imaginings as their body. Hawthorne's description figures forth the process by which any novelist conceives a fictional world, a world whose reality is neither simply subjective nor simply objective but which synthesizes elements chosen from both.

But what is peculiar about Hawthorne is that the two processes shown as blending in "The Custom-House" seem more often than not separate to him. Later in this essay he does not seem convinced by his own testimony that the imaginative act of creating a fictional world transcends the dualism of Actual and Imaginary. To choose to write *The Scarlet Letter*, he says, is to "insist on creating the semblance of a world out of airy matter"; but the

> wiser effort would have been, to diffuse thought and imagination through the opaque substance of to-day, and thus to make it a bright transparency; to spiritualize the burden that began to weigh so heavily; to seek, resolutely, the true and indestructible value that lay hidden in the petty and wearisome incidents, and ordinary characters, with which I was now conversant.

He should have done something like what the moonlight does; but—and this is what should be emphasized—the work of the moonlight and of the coal fire now seem to him antithetical, not complementary. He can choose either to give substance to his fancies or to attend imaginatively to the solid world around him, but he cannot do both. And even though, given the nature of the daily life that "The Custom-House" depicts, it is hard to agree with him that this second way would have been the wiser effort, it is highly characteristic that Hawthorne thinks so. Charles Feidelson notes that "Hawthorne had enormous respect for the material world and for common-sense reality." To this it can be added that one of the defining features of that reality is its dullness. Its incidents are petty and wearisome, its characters ordinary. Miles Coverdale seems to be expressing a tenet of his creator's metaphysics when he says of Blithedale, "when the reality comes, it will wear the every-day, common-place, dusty, and rather homely garb, that reality always does put on." And if his respect for the everyday world is partly based on an "indestructible value" that lurks in its homely appearance, it is also partly based on that world's sheer opacity, its brute actuality. As his turn against his tales in "The Old Manse" suggests, physical substance in its very physicality is of value to a man who dreads the emptiness of shadow worlds.

Given the sort of allegiance that he pays to commonsense reality, Hawthorne cannot help being hyperconscious of the gap between fact and fiction; thus in the face of his actual life in the Custom-House *The Scarlet Letter* seems to him only an airy semblance, not a real world. But, paradoxically, it is only after he has created this world of airy matter that his daily life comes to seem so full of value to him. By his own confession, he had found that existence deadening; it was only by withdrawing from its oppression of his senses that he freed his sensibilities to respond so powerfully to the scarlet letter's revelation. Because his inspiration proceeds in this way a part of Hawthorne is as hostile to the material world as another part of him is devoted to it. The sketches in *Mosses* illustrate this most clearly. It is not as if Hawthorne had aimed to endow them with richly observed external life and missed. He makes them as fantastic as possible, and he does so in order to enable them to reveal what the appearances of actual life conceal. The device of the moral lost-and-found in "The Intelligence Office" is designed to show something "truer . . . than is the living drama of action, as it evolves around us"; it dispenses with verisimilitude in order to study the essential determinant of character as a power of wish. The post-millenial tour through the relics of civilization in "A New Adam and Eve" permits him to burst "those iron fetters, which we call truth and reality" and to explore instead the psychological foundations of civil institutions. A line from "Rappaccini's Daughter" can be taken as the implicit motto of Hawthorne's anti-realistic works: "there is something truer and more real, than what we can see with the eyes, and touch with the finger." This is the truth of hidden processes, psychological and imaginative, that underlie and give shape to the apparent world; and for Hawthorne this truth is to be discovered not by trying to see into the actual but by exploring the contents of his own sensibilities.

But this position is one pole in the continuing oscillation of Hawthorne's thought, not a permanent stance. In the presence of brute actuality he comes to believe in a reality concealed by appearances and thus accessible only to the imagination; but as soon as he commits himself to the imaginative articulation of what he sees, his work comes to seem shadowy and he comes once more to consider the visible and tangible as what is really real. The conflict between these two conceptions of and approaches to reality is recapitulated in Hawthorne's theory of genres. In his definition the novelist takes as his subject "the probable and ordinary course of man's experience." He sits himself down before this reality and carefully records it; or he picks up chunks of it and puts them between the covers of a book— in an image that shows how literally he takes the connection of the novel to physical substance, Hawthorne describes Trollope's books as being "just as real as if some giant had hewn a great lump out of the earth and put it under a glass case, with all its inhabitants going about their daily business and not suspecting that they were being made a show of." The contents of the novel have their meaning by referring outward to "the actual events of real lives," by faithfully mirroring aspects of the realm of experience visible and knowable to us all. To the extent that the novel allows itself to be imaginative, and not merely a faithful record, it does so only in order to reveal a value that is seen as inhering in this experience, lying just inside its opaque substance.

By contrast romance declares its independence from the surface texture and causal order of actual life. The romance writer turns away from the world given by the senses and allows his own fantasies to come before his eyes. The world he envisions is frankly a subjective projection, but by being fully subjective it ceases to have a validity that is merely personal. By pursuing "his researches in that dusky region"—his own buried life—he can observe the operations of deep psychological forces that give shape to "our common nature." In this way romance too can claim to deal with experiential truth—not the truth of actual events but "the truth of the human heart."

How useful is this theory of genres? It seems to me that Hawthorne's strong defense of romance is achieved at the expense of an impoverished conception of the novel. He tends to forget that in the act of telling a story even the most realistic of novels organizes its presented reality into imaginative patterns of coherence and significance. His adherence to an idea of the novel as a strictly mimetic form makes him overlook its essentially fictive nature. Further, his presentation of novel and romance as antitheses implies too clear-cut a division of prose fiction into two distinct camps. Certainly his own works exemplify neither genre in a pure form. In the light of Frye's discussion of displacement it might be more helpful to understand Hawthorne's "novel" and "romance" as indicating two tendencies present and synthesized in every work of fiction, or as the end points of a whole spectrum of fictional options. Thus to the extent that a work submerges its imagined design into representations of the textures and processes of actual experience it is closer to the pole of the novel; to the extent that it orders its images of actuality into a conspicuously imagined design it is closer to the pole of romance.

But if it hampers the general theoretical validity of his definitions, Hawthorne's presentation of the novel's imaginative recording of ordinary life and romance's actualization of fantasies as mutually exclusive alternatives is in accord with the nature of his own imagination. His mind is capable of proceeding powerfully in both these directions, but it tends to work in them separately, not to merge them or mediate between them. The practical result of this habitually divided vision can be seen in the coexistence, in his novels, of solidly verisimilar and dreamily emblematic settings, of characters endowed with the large variety of overlapping attributes that compose a whole personality and spectral characters who have the reality of archetypical figures of good and evil, of actions that flow from fully dramatized relationships and actions governed by a more ghostly logic of violation and revenge. And his vision's dividedness is reinforced by his divided artistic aspirations. However much he defends romance in his prefaces, with another part of his mind he wants to achieve the novel's sort of substantiality—his description of Trollope's great lumps of earth is written with envious admiration. Hawthorne is bound to produce a mixed medium in his fiction because he will not choose one of these fictional modes at the expense of the other and he cannot see them as anything but antithetical.

But if he does not transcend or neutralize this tension within his imagination, he does, in his best work, convert this tension into an artistic asset. The way of the novel and the way of romance are not, for him, simply two methods to pick and choose between. As his theoretical statements show, he thinks of each of them as corresponding to a particular conception of the nature of reality and as being capable of rendering a particular sort of experiential truth. And although it might seem from the preface to *The House of the Seven Gables* that he is content to settle back and accept both these modes as valid in their own ways, this should be understood as a temporary stance, not Hawthorne's last word. What we have seen of his habitual oscillation between them suggests that it is more characteristic for him to see the claims of these modes as conflicting and competing; the nature of their validity is a subject of constant and anxious reformulation, not of settled opinion. Within his novels this question is emphatically an open one. All of them are experiments in which he allows each kind of vision to create its own fictional reality and explores, in the context of the specific experience that is the work's subject, the sort of truth that each of them can articulate.

Hawthorne's unwillingness or inability to abjure the rough magic of romance keeps his novels from fully achieving the "physical substance enough to stand alone" that he had at first desired for them. But by bringing his own discontinuous modes of vision into meaningful relationships he is able to keep the spirit of his resolution at the Old Manse even as he violates its letter. By this means as he undertakes his large and serious treatment of human experience his fictional form acts out a drama appropriate to that subject. It holds open court on the question of how experience is best visualized and understood.

Family Discourse and Fiction in *The Scarlet Letter*

Michael Ragussis

"Speak; and give your child a father!"

Hawthorne and his characters imagine speech as an act of potency. But the ban of silence lies on everyone in *The Scarlet Letter*. The act of speech is baffled during the entire course of the tale, suppressed from without and repressed from within, until the confession at the end when the minister comes forth to speak and turns into the father. I must add immediately that the source of what I am calling the ban of silence lies not where we might suppose, with the Puritan censors: in fact, the Puritans issue the command to speak, calling Hester forward to utter the name of her fellow transgressor. The paralyzing silence in *The Scarlet Letter* originates with its four family members, in such acts as Hester's refusal to name Pearl's father, or Chillingworth's command that Hester swear an oath of silence, or Hester's refusal to explain to Pearl the meaning of the scarlet letter. With the acts of engendering and speech under lock and key, silence becomes a kind of action, potent to obscure, violate, and orphan. The tale's center, then, lies less in the crime of sexual transgression than in the crime of silence: to recognize publicly one's kindred is, after all, the moral concomitant to engendering, the way in which family is defined not merely biologically but morally. My examination of the silence that prevents those acts of speech that name and identify the family member leads logically, in

From *ELH* 49, no. 4 (Winter 1982). © 1982 by The Johns Hopkins University Press.

the second half of this essay, to the question of how fiction is a mode of discourse based on the family. I do not mean simply that fiction is a language enlisted from the outside to tell what the family will not tell, but that fiction is a revision of those acts of speech and silence whereby the family makes and unmakes itself.

The way in which Hester's refusal to speak Dimmesdale's name in the marketplace frustrates her simple desire to protect him, and then threatens her child and herself, dramatizes most clearly the dangerous effects of silence. In Dimmesdale's call to Hester to name her fellow criminal ("What can thy silence do for him, except it tempt him—yea, compel him, as it were—to add hypocrisy to sin?") and in his description of the pain of hiding a guilty heart through life, we see how Hester's silence becomes a curious punishment more than equal to what the Puritan authorities would require of her lover. In Pearl's apparently tautological description of herself, "I am mother's child," we see a half-truth, actually a dangerous misunderstanding that means there is no father: the mother's silence is an analogue of what we usually take to be the stern Puritan censor, misinforming the child by obscuring the act of engendering. Finally, when Hester later wonders where Pearl came from (even to the point of denying the child is her own), we see how her refusal to name the father grows into self-mystification, robbing her of her motherhood notwithstanding the fact that she has a child. Adultery is a crime against society, but Hester's silence begins to look like a crime against nature. The child engendered by one parent alone and the virgin mother are not members of the human family as we know it.

The ban of silence appropriately begins when all four family members are brought together for the first time. The first act that the reader sees Chillingworth perform is an act that silences another: the physician raises his finger and lays it on his lips, gesturing Hester not to reveal his identity. This gesture of silence precedes, only by moments, Hester's crucial act in the same chapter: "Madam Hester absolutely refuseth to speak." Hester's silence is, of course, meant to protect Dimmesdale, but Hawthorne begins at this point to show us a strange complicity between the two men. At first, of course, Dimmesdale seems Chillingworth's opposite because the minister appears to be asking Hester to reveal his identity, to name him as her fellow criminal. But Dimmesdale's speech is equal to Chillingworth's silence. He calls on Hester to speak, but he delights in her silence: "Wondrous strength and generosity of a woman's heart! She will not speak!" Hester's silence, then, hides the identities of both men, or what amounts to the same thing in this text, their familial relationship to her and her child. At the same time this silence begins a new bond: silence obfuscates the differences between husband and lover. The two are one in their single desire—to have the woman remain silent.

The events I have just described Hawthorne places side by side in the chapter shrewdly entitled "The Recognition." Hawthorne has in mind here the Aristotelian idea of *anagnorisis*, or "the change from ignorance to knowledge of a bond of love or hate." In *The Scarlet Letter* the obfuscated and persistently delayed recognition of enemy and kindred—another way, for both Hawthorne and Aristotle, of putting the dichotomy between "hatred and love"—is the source of the prolonged suffering of each of the family members. In this light the entire narrative of *The Scarlet Letter* depends on whatever hinders or hastens the central issue from the start—"Speak out the name!" In "The Recognition" no recognitions are made public, and even those that occur are unrealized in the deepest sense. When Dimmesdale requests that Hester speak the name of Pearl's father, for example, the power of his voice almost gives him away to his child, "for it [the poor baby] directed its hitherto vacant gaze towards Mr. Dimmesdale, and held up its little arms." But the blood-bond is not publicly recognized. It is instead painfully pictured in the child's helpless gesture toward her hidden father. The child unable to speak is at the mercy of adult hypocrisy, false words and names. In fact the chapter closes with a silencing of the child that, with Hester's silence over Dimmesdale and Chillingworth, brings all four family members under the same tragic cover of silence: "The infant . . . pierced the air with its wailing and screams; she [Hester] strove to hush it, mechanically, but seemed scarcely to sympathize with its trouble."

"The Recognition" ends with mother and child once again disappearing behind the "iron-clamped portal" of the Puritan jail, but now we understand the way in which the self is incarcerated within the walls of its own silence. The text deliberately connects silence and symbolic imprisonment, explaining how Chillingworth possesses "the lock and key of her [Hester's] silence." Hester is imprisoned in this way in "The Interview" (the chapter following "The Recognition"), where the power of speech is subverted, to be used in the service of silence. Chillingworth replaces the blood-bond with the "secret bond" not to speak—Hester's slavish bondage, her "oath" to silence. The prison of silence is equal to his repetition of the suffocating command "Breathe not." The silence Hester keeps in order to protect her lover merges with the silence that prevents him from discovering the identity of his worst enemy. If speech is the medium for recognizing the difference between kindred and enemy, silence dissolves the difference between the real father and the evil father-surrogate or "enemy." The family drama of *The Scarlet Letter* is played out between the subverted recognitions I have just described and the recognition scene that occurs between child and father at the end. But, as I will show in the following pages, with a child consistently hushed, and educated in the family language by her mother and the Puritan authorities, and with a father who, even when he speaks the truth, transforms it into falsehood, the denouement of the tale is delayed.

The crying infant hushed mechanically by its mother becomes the child learning to speak, but in this apparent progression we learn how the methods of silence are merely refined. When Mr. Wilson asks Pearl who she is, he seems to be rephrasing, without the sharp edge of command, the earlier declaration that Hester speak. But we soon see that the apparently open question is a disguised command to answer by the book. The question of the child's identity is persistently reshaped by an inevitable corollary: Mr. Wilson first asks Pearl "who art thou?" and then "Canst thou tell me, my child, who made thee?" It is essentially the same question asked Hester, but now Mr. Wilson wants a different answer—not the earthly father, but the Heavenly Father. In this way Mr. Wilson inadvertently contributes to Hester's hiding of the father. The child is viewed as the product of a mysterious and contradictory process in which her maker is either spiritual or biological, or—worse—indiscriminately both. In Pearl's case, both answers are incomprehensible; both fathers are absent, invisible, bodiless.

Pearl's refusal to name "the Heavenly Father" as her maker is, stated baldly, a refusal to name Him, the unnameable source of her being, that "Creator of all Flesh" who is fleshless himself. The Heavenly Father here seems at once an idealized and ironic double of the earthly father who neglects to name Pearl, and who, after engendering her, disappears from the flesh. She might as well invent her identity, since she seems an invention, a fanciful unreality: "the child finally announced that she had not been made at all, but had been plucked by her mother off the bush of wild roses, that grew by the prison-door." The fatherless and lawless child appropriately provides her own genealogy according to no law we can understand, as if she were a freak of nature, either engendered by one parent alone or plucked from a rose bush.

Pearl's mother questions the child's origin by repeating the pattern of Mr. Wilson's questions: "Tell me, then, what thou art, and who sent thee hither." The mother's puzzlement over who made the child—Pearl's own identity is consistently displaced in the search for another's—reaches its farthest point when Hester questions even the immediate and visible bond that is the child's only certain knowledge: "Child, what art thou? . . . Art thou my child, in very truth?" Hester actually disowns Pearl "half playfully" in what must be a bad joke: "Thou art not my child!" Both father and mother, then, deny Pearl her source. For these reasons the name the mother bestows, the child's other source of certain identity, becomes the locus of abuse and displacement, and a way of disqualifying Pearl's human nature, for even Pearl's mother "could not help questioning whether Pearl was a human child." Pearl is identified through a series of "ill name[s]" that place in quarantine the child who is so avoided she must be considered contagious: she is a "demon offspring," an "imp of evil," an "airy sprite," and a "little elf." We will momentarily see that what Pearl suffers—not being allowed a human name because of her mysterious origin—Chillingworth wills for himself (without realizing the consequences) when he "chose to withdraw his name from the roll of mankind." Finally, unnamed by her father and ill-named by the community, the child is renamed by Mr. Wilson. He objects to the child's answer to his question "who are thou?" by arguing with her name: judging by appearances she should be named "Ruby" or "Coral" or "Red Rose"—more names that deny her a human engendering. Such are the liberties taken with an unnamed bastard: Mr. Wilson knows better than the child who made her and knows the child's proper name. Pearl's life is specified far outside herself, and her name seems an ironic tease. Mr. Wilson calls her "my child" (has *he* made her?), but she appears to belong to no one. As a bastard, she is a counterfeit pearl, disowned by father and mother alike.

The questions that both Mr. Wilson and Hester direct at Pearl, and the ironic corrections of the child's name, are part of an educative system that confounds the issue of personal identity. The social authorities, as I have already implied, "analyze . . . the child's nature" to find the perpetrator of the crime she represents, and "put the child to due and stated examination" solely to prove and insure their own beliefs. In such ways the child's life is posited outside itself, and questioned from the outside by a catechism whose questions are hypocritical at worst, rhetorical at best. The child-puppet must give another's answers: Pearl's "one baby-voice served a multitude of imaginary personages." Pearl's attempt to ask her own questions is limited by a system that allows only two kinds of questions—those that have a priori answers (like "the Heavenly Father") and those that should not be asked at all: "There are many things in this world that a child must not ask about." Nevertheless Pearl appears in the text, time and again, as an almost disembodied string of questions that have been prohibited: "[S]he put these searching questions, once, and again, and still a third time . . . What does the letter mean?—and why dost thou wear it?—and why does the minister keep his hand over his heart?" Such questions are part of the child's native understanding that it is her prerogative to ask, and that the mother (not the child) should explain the scarlet letter: "It is thou that must tell me!" "Tell me, mother! . . . Do thou tell me!" When Hester answers that she wears the scarlet letter "for the sake of its gold thread," the narrator marks one of those turning points in the text where the ostensible crime (the sexual transgression) shrinks beside a more profound one: "In all the seven bygone years, Hester Prynne had never before been false to the symbol on her bosom. . . . [S]ome new evil had crept into her heart, or some old one had never been expelled."

The lie about the letter is so serious because it breaks the sacred bond through which the mother teaches the child the alphabet that articulates her identity and her place in the human community. Hester is, in the educative system I am describing, the teacher of the mother tongue, as Pearl herself acknowledges—"It is the great letter A. Thou hast taught it me in the hornbook." Hester's refusal to inform the child of the letter's greater, or at least special, significance makes the child fail her examination in the simplest of categories, the ABC's of who she is. Hester's final answer to Pearl's questions is a command to be silent, which equals shutting the child away—"Hold thy tongue . . . else I shall shut thee into the dark closet!"—returning her to the dark unknown from which she came, denying her here and now, refusing her any existence at all. Not allowed her own questions, kept from the meaning of the letter *A*, Pearl is reduced either to a perverse silence (self-hushed with a vengeance) or to an incomprehensible language unable to bear or articulate the burden of her pain and rage: a "perversity . . . closed her lips, or impelled her to speak words amiss . . . putting her finger in her mouth"; "If spoken to, she would not speak again," or would rush forth "with shrill, incoherent exclamations that made her mother tremble, because they had so much the sound of a witch's anathemas in some unknown tongue."

The child's relentless but unsatisfied questions, and the mother's taunting questions and answers about the letter, tease Pearl to the quick because, as Hawthorne insists, the child is in fact "the scarlet letter endowed with life!" Pearl is a baffling linguistic equation come alive: "She had been offered to the world, these seven years past, as the living hieroglyphic, in which was revealed the secret they so darkly sought to hide,—all written in this symbol,—all plainly manifest,—had there been a prophet or magician skilled to read the character of flame!" The letter shows Pearl as a contradiction, a language whose meaning is at once self-apparent and mystifyingly in need of being read by another. With Pearl as the letter, Hawthorne chooses to show us the most painful way in which the self depends upon another—namely, through the child who carries her own meaning conceived as another's. Pearl is divided from the meaning she is equal to—whether staring at the mirroring brook, experiencing herself as another (as if her identity resides in a mysteriously impalpable image outside herself), or trying to understand her life conceived as a linguistic equation whose first term—the letter *A*—she is unable to read, and worse still, not allowed to read. The child's identity is conceived as another's: that is, as a letter, she is a clue to the full reading of another's identity—*A* is an abbreviation for Adultery, even for Arthur, while the first two letters of adultery are the initials of the father. Pearl, as the first initial of some hidden word or name, is an abbreviated form of her father, just as the face she sees in the mirroring brook (as Dimmesdale fears) traces her father's features and is thereby capable of revealing him as Hester's fellow transgressor. Finally, Pearl is a living hieroglyphic or abbreviation because she is made out of her parents' linguistic half-truths and deceptions. To deny the facts of Pearl's biological making, to deny that she is their own child, is to transform her into a disembodied linguistic conundrum, as Hester's experience shows: "the mother felt like one who has evoked a spirit, but, by some irregularity in the process of conjuration, has failed to win the master-word that should control this new and incomprehensible intelligence." Hester sees herself as a wizard-scientist who fails to understand the monster-spirit she has conjured, but she (like the father) has in her own keeping the master-word that will make Pearl human.

The letter as an unreadable abbreviation of a human life is the most appropriate sign of Pearl's half-life because a letter or a child is, in isolation, a sign divorced from meaning, in need of definition through others. A letter and a child are trapped in a past each is ignorant of, a history of meanings that in turn delimit individual meaning, my meaning. Each depends upon an authorizing context which, in Pearl's case, is hidden. For this reason Pearl, like a symbolic letter, becomes a battleground of meaning—between parents, society, and heaven. Pearl has only a representative meaning: she is "meant, above all things else, to keep the mother's soul alive." In fact Pearl is a prize to be won, a bargain between two beings outside herself, a middle term, even a test case. Her daughter is supposed to remind Hester that "if she bring the child to heaven, the child also will bring its parent thither!" But for the mother, Pearl is as well a constant reminder of her sin and shame, just as for the father who fears he will be traced in his child's features. Pearl is the only visible clue that links him to his crime. Because the child—like the scarlet letter—is the public sign of their most private acts, the parents try to obscure its meaning by hushing it or simply refusing it, denying that it is their own. Such acts become criminal when we realize the way in which meaning becomes human, the way in which the child is the letter endowed with life.

When we are told, "in this one child there were many children," we see the statement means two things: first, that Pearl is divided from herself, splintered; and second, that the child, the character at the center of the text, is a multiple reflection of all the characters in *The Scarlet Letter*. The child, reduced to a mere fleshless symbol of itself (like the image of Pearl in the brook, or the ghostly disembodiments that Dimmesdale and Hester undergo), is a helpless creature in another's control—denied meaning by others (mastered by another's master-words and silences), living in fear of the incomprehensibility of another. At the same time, the process of conjuration, like that of engendering, shows us that the creator's magic backfires. The control we think we exert over another often produces a new, incomprehensible, and uncontrollable intelligence. Hence Pearl is a "deadly symbol," the letter that killeth. Pearl's mere gaze at the letter on her mother's breast, for example, is "like the stroke of sudden death." In the person of the child the letter becomes a vengeful literalism that strikes through guise and deceit. For the child, despite all the methods of parental and societal control exerted on it, represents an alien other to be feared, and one who—though we may deny it—we in fact produce ourselves.

To move from Pearl's fate to Dimmesdale's is to see how one depends on the other. But the child owns us as much as we own it: the father cannot be himself until he acknowledges his child. Dimmesdale's identity, too, rests on a linguistic deadlock that makes for the durance, and duration, of the tale. On the one hand, neither Pearl's nor Chillingworth's guesses, nor Hester's betrayal of his name, will solve the riddle of the father's identity. The father must speak for himself. On the other hand, Dimmesdale's life fluctuates between two linguistic poles—between asking another to speak for him and speaking for another; this makes solving the riddle impossible. I take this characteristic of Dimmesdale's speech to be the central symptom of a "disorder in his utterance" that Chillingworth, for all his probing of the minister's illness, fails to recognize. By asking another to speak for him and thereby name him, Dimmesdale childishly places his identity outside himself, at the mercy of another. Hester of course protects him, and refuses his plea to name her fellow transgressor, but even she eventually tries renaming him (the way Mr. Wilson tries changing Pearl into "Ruby"). She does not realize that to "give up this name of Arthur Dimmesdale, and make thyself another . . . thou canst wear," would be to make the minister more lost to himself, and one step closer to another "wearer" of false names, Roger Chillingworth. When not asking another to name him, Dimmesdale himself speaks for another: speaking for Hester (she later commands him, "Speak thou for me!") is like speaking for his flock generally, or for his God. In this way Dimmesdale becomes a selfless medium, his own voice in another's body or someone else's voice in his body. Such transgressions, meant to hide his crime, only repeat it. As "the mouth-piece of Heaven's messages," he is like the puppet-child, a linguistic tool given up to represent another's meaning. In fact, just as Pearl is equal to the scarlet letter, Dimmesdale is equal to his voice, to his utterance. While Dimmesdale rightly wonders "that Heaven should see fit to transmit the grand and solemn music of its oracles through so foul an organ-pipe as he," Hawthorne makes the equation clear. It is not simply mouth, throat, or tongue that Heaven takes over as its conduit, but the whole man, "he." And yet the minister's function as a medium is a useful hiding place that obviates his speaking for himself, being his own person. The father actually courts obfuscation and misrepresentation, and turns those acts that endanger the child—being unnamed or misread or silenced—to his own purposes. His utterances are part of a system of counterspeech where even the truth becomes a hiding place, a deception: "The minister well knew—subtle, but remorseful hypocrite that he was!—the light in which his vague confession would be viewed. . . . He had spoken the very truth, and transformed it into the veriest falsehood." To speak double, to intend the opposite of what your words say, repeats the strategy behind his request that Hester reveal his identity.

Such speech acts, like his passion, "hurrieth him out of himself," and thereby show his complete confusion over self and other. The minister eventually moves to the opposite extreme, and by speaking only to himself he literalizes—and unwittingly parodies—the idea of speaking for himself. He imagines speeches (in "The Minister's Vigil" and "The Minister in a Maze") that are in fact never spoken. The self makes itself an audience and attempts recognition without the aid of another. These speeches, spoken only on the inside, completely dispense with other people and divide the self in two—that is, they make Dimmesdale "another" in yet another way. They are a narcissistic self-communication, a misconstrued lesson learned from Dimmesdale's sexual transgression, a false antidote to intercourse with another. Speech, like the self it grounds, has become mere hallucination, mere fantasy. The father works himself like a puppet.

The equivocal status of Dimmesdale's identity—the way in which he seems both to court obfuscation and yet to suffer from the very acts of speech that make him over into another—is most sharply expressed when he poses for the entire community the "riddle" of Oedipal identity. In the marketplace Dimmesdale, like Oedipus, calls for the solution of the crime he himself has committed. Knowing that he is the man everyone (himself included) seeks, he is at once a criminal and a hypocrite, a knowing Oedipus. Nonetheless his knowledge of his own identity turns out to be, in substantial ways, incomplete: he, like the child, depends on another. Dimmesdale does not realize that the physician is cast, in this complicated family drama, in the role of the minister's father, with the old man's feigned "paternal and reverential love for the young pastor" an ironic echo of the true father's refusal to come forth and love Pearl. Dimmesdale's accusation of Chillingworth, the father-substitute—"You speak in riddles"—names the crime he himself commits. What Pearl suffers—the painful riddle of the father's identity—is now turned on him. He has a "nameless horror" of the father-substitute whose namelessness becomes the source of a deadly riddle; "he could not recognize his enemy" in a drama where he withholds recognition from his own flesh-and-blood kin.

Neither Dimmesdale nor Chillingworth realizes that the self disguised, the self that prevents another from recognizing it, is the self lost through the very process of self-defense. Dimmesdale's double failure—to recognize Pearl and to recognize Chillingworth—is part of a single confusion: the deliberate failure to recognize one's kindred merges with the involuntary failure to discover the enemy. When Chillingworth catches in the mirror a grotesquely evil image of himself "which he could not recognize," he doubly represents Dimmesdale—neither man can recognize the leech, neither man can recognize himself (as the enemy). The attack against the simple and easily identifiable enemy becomes the attack against the family member, and ultimately self-attack. The question about the enemy (Dimmesdale asks about Chillingworth, "Who is he? Who is he?") merges with the question about oneself (Chillingworth asks about Dimmesdale, "Who is he?"). It is the same question asked about the child, the same question I ask about myself—and for this reason it is first asked in the autobiographical sketch as the question Hawthorne's forefathers ask about him ("What is he?"), and therefore as the motivating force of Hawthorne's entire fiction.

The father's refusal to recognize his real child leads to his production of a mock child—to his engendering the enemy in and by himself. In this light Pearl (the child) and Chillingworth (the enemy) play a similar role. Both seek to expose Dimmesdale's secret: both ask him leading questions, both frighten him, both riddle him (see, for example, Pearl's teasing mock exposure of Chillingworth's identity in an unknown tongue that puzzles her father). But who is Chillingworth anyway, and why do his questions often coincide with Pearl's? The man "Chillingworth" comes into being only because of Dimmesdale's and Hester's passion: he is as much their child as the unclaimed Pearl. In fact, as the leech, he is the man completely and grotesquely "dependent for the food of his affections and spiritual life upon another," a child dependent on Dimmesdale for the pound of flesh he exacts. Or to put it another way: the "devil" Chillingworth is an example of the guilty offspring produced by men who "propagate a hellish breed within them[selves]." The question asked Pearl, "who made thee?" Chillingworth asks about himself, mystified by the new demonic identity he sees in the mirror: "Who made me so?" But while the text persuasively shows how the self is dependent on another, Chillingworth functions as a limit to this idea: he is responsible for himself (even as he allows himself to become completely dependent on Dimmesdale). One could argue that the two men reciprocally produce each other: like Dimmesdale's guilt, Chillingworth's revenge produces the enemy. The real child Pearl is lost among the shadow-children produced in these mock engenderings. But then Pearl learns to play the same game: she engenders her own dummy "offspring," "puppets" who are nameless and passive victims held in the child-parent's power. The child repeats the way in which she is displaced—through mock engendering and the view of the offspring as the "enem[y]."

The family member frames and limits my life, but in what sense he assumes the publicly recognized, or even literal, relationship of kindred is another matter; he is a sign, like *A*, with too many significations. Family titles, one could argue, are linguistic shifters, like the pronoun "he" that alternately represents Dimmesdale, Chillingworth, and Hawthorne himself: they relativize the single substantial name (which, in this text, is already a ghostly sign, if not a downright lie). The titles "parent" and "child," for example, shift both literally (the text carefully shows us both Hester and Dimmesdale as children by showing us their parents) and symbolically (with Chillingworth as the product of Hester's and Dimmesdale's passion, or of Dimmesdale's guilt; with Hester as Dimmesdale's mother, when he walks with "the wavering effort of an infant, with its mother's arms in view"; with Pearl as the parent of her play–offspring, or an "authority" over Hester and Dimmesdale). The family's acts of silence unwittingly bring such meanings to the surface, and reveal that the deepest family discourse—not the one the world finds acceptable—casts the family member in every role, including that of enemy. The letter of the law tries to control such meanings, to fix such titles as "father" and "husband" and "child," but the scarlet letter, as it exhausts the single meaning the law attaches to it, exhausts such controls generally. It is the badge every family member wears.

The sexual act lies outside the narrative not because of some peculiar

Puritanical censor at work in Hawthorne, but because the family itself redefines engenderment. Hawthorne shows the family as the creator of its own system of suppression, torture, and violation. This is the deepest meaning of engenderment in *The Scarlet Letter*—the violation and death the family makes for itself. In *The Scarlet Letter*, the family sees fall before its own eyes the mythology that divides enemy from kindred, other from self—a mythology that every family makes itself. In this light the search after the identity of Pearl's father, after his proper name and the child's, is foiled not simply because of the particular acts of secrecy and deception performed by particular family members, but because it is in the nature of families, and the self they define, not to allow such literal, fixed, or single names. For such reasons the text postpones through its entirety answering the literal questions the community asks. Who is the father, or for that matter, who the child? What is the crime, and who the criminal? Who is *he*?

The foregoing discussion of silence and speech, and of parent and child, is open to the charge of being incomplete. I have neglected Dimmesdale's confession, the speech that gives the child her father. Moreover, I have neglected to say that the acts of silence (and counterspeech) that make up the action of the tale are anticipated and framed by the author's own analogous acts. In the first sentence of the text Hawthorne is "taken possession of," against his natural instincts and perhaps better judgment, by an autobiographical urge to speak. At the beginning of "The Custom-House" he hesitates and cautions himself in a stop-and-start-again style almost paralyzed by interrupting dashes (six occur in the first two sentences alone) and limiting conjunctions ("but" and "though" and "however") that reroute the direction of his desire: to speak or not to speak. What finally allows him to write this autobiographical preface is the carefully rehearsed set of checks and balances that becomes its subtext—namely, cautions about speaking, while speaking. The strictures are clear: a "decorous" and "modest" style of a man who does not want to become "the intrusive author"; a writer who is ever ready to "plead guilty" to his mistakes, to avoid "violating either the reader's rights or his own"—Hawthorne lays down "the law of literary propriety" that makes speaking "pardonable." To be silent, to hide your name and history from the text of your writing, is to repeat the father's criminal acts of silence, concealment, and abandonment. To speak, to probe and expose another, to unveil oneself in public, is to repeat the speech act that violates—that is, to be at once another's and your own enemy. My excuse for postponing both the father's confession and the author's halting autobiographical start stems from my effort to underscore a significant structural device of the text—namely, how the confession at the end (postponed by the narrative itself) turns us back to the prefatory essay, where we find Hawthorne's desire "[t]o confess the truth" and the complex desires and laws that possess the author himself in the contest between speech and silence. Dimmesdale is given another double, Hawthorne himself, and the author seems to know already from the start the lesson the reader will learn: namely, that both silence and speech can be criminal acts. But this knowledge hardly saves him from their dangers.

When we take a careful look at Dimmesdale's confession and Hawthorne's autobiographical sketch, we begin to see how both, apparently the most sincere acts in the text, might better be termed fictions. The minister's confession holds the key here. Dimmesdale is so much at the center of this text because he exaggerates, to the point of madness, a universal ambivalence: he at once dreads discovery and longs for it. Confession, rather than solving this painful contradiction, underscores it. But Dimmesdale's fictionalized confession protects him at the same time that it lets him speak the truth and reveal who he is.

In *The Scarlet Letter*, confession occurs paradoxically through a process of apparent self-alienation and fiction. During his public confession, Dimmesdale (like a novelist) speaks of himself in the third person: "But there stood one in the midst of you, at whose brand of sin and infamy ye have not shuddered! . . . It was on him! . . . But he hid it cunningly from men, and walked among you. . . . Now, at the death-hour, he stands up before you! He bids you look at Hester's scarlet letter! He tells you, that, with all its mysterious horror, it is but the shadow of what he bears on his own breast, and that even this, his own red stigma, is no more than the type of what has seared his inmost heart." Who is the secret man the minister speaks of? The minister's truest moment, when he is most himself, is a moment of self-alienation, of ghostly autobiography and confession: it shows the self in a mirror, as "he." Appropriately, the man the minister names (or does not name) as "he" answers the question that has echoed through the text: "What is he?"(the forefathers ask about Hawthorne); "Who is he?"(Chillingworth asks about Dimmesdale); "Then, what was he?" (the narrator asks about Dimmesdale); "Who is he? Who is he?"(Dimmesdale asks about Chillingworth). "He" is the man who walks always beside you, unrecognized. Dimmesdale finally becomes the "exemplary man" in an unexpected way—not through his virtue but through his power of representation. A man dramatizes himself, to himself and others, as another; he makes himself visible, to himself and others, in a reflection, or a representation that is fictional; he/"he" tells the truth.

The fiction of Dimmesdale's confession, as I understand it, is defined in opposition to *The Scarlet Letter*'s view of writing in general. Writing is a form of literalization that puts the blame simply and mercilessly on another: the text's powerful example here is the way in which the Puritans use writing to label Hester. Fiction, on the other hand, is a more generous and complicated form of what Hawthorne in another context sees as "the propensity of human nature to tell the very worst of itself, when embodied in the person of another"—in other words, to confess as "he," like Dimmesdale or like a novelist. There is a discrimination here that will become clearer as my argument proceeds, but let me immediately try to clarify my terms, admitting that while writing and fiction are close doubles, the slightest discrimination makes all the difference—between branding and casting out a single victim, and accusing an unspecified person who walks among you; between depersonalization as attack (writing's criminal is the Adulteress, the dehumanized Hester) and impersonalization as merciful defense (fiction's criminal is an unnamed "he"). Writing violates, with a sharp-edged instrument; fiction deflects and defends, with a language that shows that pain and guilt are common to all. These are the two ways the two criminals of adultery are named in the text: one is named by another at the beginning of the text, while one is named as another by himself at the end of the text. The first is an object of scorn set apart from all others; the second is "he" conceived as the invisible self that we all share but fail to recognize.

In writing (as in the simplified discourse families use) you accuse another in place of yourself; the confusion over self and other is too easily solved by labelling the other a criminal. But Hawthorne shows that this kind of writing is itself a crime. Reduced to a "text," "giving up her individuality, she [Hester] would become the general symbol at which the preacher and moralist might point, and in which they might vivify and embody their images of woman's frailty and sinful passion." Text and symbol vivify and embody, but at great cost—they mortify and feed off Hester in a further example of the text's view of the parasite or leech. Writing as embodiment takes over the body to make it a symbolic representation, "the body . . . of sin." As writers, the Puritans are "iron men" who use the equipment of their apparent antitype, the Black man. The "iron pen" violates and thereby engenders the body of sin (repeating the crime it punishes): Hester's cry is that she has been "too deeply branded," just as Hawthorne himself complains of the "deep print" in his brain which he cannot erase, the product of the self-mortification that lies behind the tale of his ancestors' crime. In the same movement the iron pen imprisons the body of sin it has made, and labels it for all to see. It makes violation and shame public, and this is the most scandalous side of writing. Puritan society, in its search after visible truths in signs, types, and tokens, consistently errs on the side of literalism. The Puritans, in a theological confusion of the Pauline distinction between letter and spirit, transfer the letter of the law from the tables of stone to the fleshy tables of the heart. In this way their writing makes Hester's heart into a dead stone, a "tomb-like heart." The letter is her epitaph, and Hester as a living text or sermon is a dead woman awaiting burial: "Thus she will be a living sermon against sin, until the ignominious letter be engraved upon her tombstone." The letter on her heart is a proleptic sign that from the beginning seeks fulfillment in the story's final writing, the letter written on the gravestone. The letter is the sign of the "ministration of death, written and engraved in stone" (2 Cor. 3:7). Fiction becomes defined against this system of writing—in fact, in order to elude the kind of writing that is part of that "penal machine" in which the gripe "forbid[s] the culprit to hide his face for shame." Fiction discovers that "neutral territory" (Hawthorne's term for the border "where the Actual and Imaginary may meet") where it is safe to confess, where you neither label yourself nor are labelled by another: in fiction you speak the truth in the third person.

The scarlet letter itself helps clarify the difference between writing and fiction precisely in so far as it resists the (literal) function the Puritans assign it. In this way it becomes the key to writing's failure when writing tries to fix meaning. The letter's meaning is knotted, intertwined, a complete mesh not to be unravelled. This is why Hawthorne tells us that its art cannot be reproduced or analyzed, "even by the process of picking out the threads." The scarlet letter turns against its Puritan authors by revealing the judges' failure at "disentangling . . . [the] mesh of good and evil"; it understands the complexity of human action by showing characters who "continually did one thing or another, which intertwined, in the same inextricable knot." The "margin" or "edge" or "verge" where Dimmesdale and Chillingworth and even Hawthorne the writer live, and where Pearl plays, is a knotted or entangled world, an Adulterated world where all things are alloyed. The alchemical search to "distil," to separate out the "residuum," to have the soul "dissolved, and flow forth in a . . . transparent stream," is foiled in a world in which things are "intermingled," "thoroughly interfused," in an "admixture of . . . ingredients." For this reason Pearl (or the letter she is) reminds us of a "necessity that always impelled this child to alloy whatever comfort she might chance to give with a throb of anguish." *A* stands for such adultery—for the knot, the margin, the alloy. It suggests a complex moral world that resists a Manichean unraveling of good and evil, a simple alchemical distillation of value. Adultery, in this light, is at once an act that lies outside the law of Puritan society, and a meaning that explodes the limits of writing.

With this definition before us, the adulterous self is the self I share with another—not necessarily through sexual trespass, but through a marginality that stems from the beginning: A stands for Adultery at the beginning, for the impossibility of finding an unadulterated origin. The text's adulterations are interpolations between epochs, made most patent in the formal movement between the contemporary events of the Custom-House and Puritan New England. The self is an adulterated compound because it exists "across the gulf of time," "across the verge of time": "This victim was for ever on the rack," stretched between times. This is another way of saying that the self is familial, that it contains the genealogical trace or blood-guilt of its ancestry. The man Chillingworth is "[m]isshapen from birth" and seeks the "veil" that will disguise his "physical deformity": the physician's disguise here becomes the object of our mercy. Even Dimmesdale's crime of passion can be referred, at least in part, to someone or something before him: he "inherited a strong animal nature from his father or his mother." The family member, then, is not only the person found on the border of another in his present family relations; he is also the person who is a "residuum" or "diluted repetition" or "vestige" of the ancestors that went before him. This is what it means to be a daughter or son, all one's life. The mark on Dimmesdale's breast is the scarlet letter with a particular or literal meaning: Dimmesdale is the man who committed adultery, even as the law defines it. But the mark on his breast is also the universal mark of all men born of woman—"the natal spot."

The idea of the adulterous self—the self that is mixed with another, from the beginning—explains Hawthorne's skepticism about autobiographical speech. Then why preface the tale with an autobiographical sketch? Because, as the analogue to the minister's confession in the third person, the autobiographical sketch fictionalizes the first person. "The Custom-House" exists, at the head of the text, to warn us from the beginning that it does not want to speak the entire truth about the self, nor could it even if it wanted to. It exists to subvert itself, to fictionalize itself deliberately before its own eyes and the reader's. In this light we begin to realize that both sections of this text are alloys: can we distinguish between the truth of autobiography and the fiction of the tale by saying which event—Hawthorne's discovery of Pue's papers or the death of Governor Winthrop—belongs to which half of the text? The autobiographical sketch is a series of clues and red herrings left at the scene of the crime. Its most blatant lie, Hawthorne's explanation that he is not the author but an editor who has accidentally found the story of the scarlet letter, is a repetition of Dimmesdale's criminal concealment, a casting off of the child, a withholding of the father's name. But such a lie reveals a truth that we discover is the heart of the tale as well. Above all, the lie understands the self's need to be defended against writing's tendency to literalize; against its own urge to label itself and to assert itself as a subject, against the egotism of thinking itself a first cause. The lie shows that what we call the subject, or in this case the author, is a fiction, as Hawthorne suggests elsewhere: "A person to be writing a tale, and to find that it shapes itself against his intentions; that the characters act otherwise than he thought; that unforeseen events occur, and a catastrophe which he strives in vain to avert. It might shadow forth his own fate—he having made himself one of the personages." The autobiographical sketch makes the author a character (just as the tale does): the man who finds and edits Pue's papers is a fictitious character who nevertheless reveals the truth about "the author" Hawthorne. The autobiographical preface rests on this paradox, then—that it tells the truth through an oblique and fictionalized attack on the idea of the subject, through an understanding that the self (even when a father or an author) is at least in part the product of another's making. Hawthorne's reminder that "both truth and error" can coexist in a single impression becomes a warning that the opposites the text contemplates—kindred and enemy, love and hatred, good and evil—and their literary coordinates, autobiography and fiction, author and character—are so many different ways of repeating the same mythical search for purity, the same naive unravelling of self and other. Read in this way, "The Custom-House" bestows upon "I" and "he" the function of doubles, where no one is prior or original: we can use either to hide ourselves, either to confess the truth about ourselves.

The fiction in Dimmesdale's confession and in Hawthorne's autobiography is not solely a practical psychological defense. It is as well a moral critique of the categorical opposites I have just listed. Fiction understands that the most radical name we bestow upon the self, the name that in fact logically follows from "author" and "subject," is "the criminal." The idea of the criminal stems from the false differences the self ascribes to another, the way the self writes him off: we mark him clearly so that we can safely stay away from him. But he is, as my string of associations suggests (the author, the autobiographical subject), the other side of myself. Based on a darker and more threatening view of the self as a first cause, the term "criminal" shows us how the idea of the subject backfires: it can be used against me. By showing the family as a tangle of crimes where kindred and enemy often change places, Hawthorne shows how criminal and victim are one, with each member of the family on both sides of the border of crime. In this light the way in which we typically define the self merges with the discourse of the family: the reified self is the subject-author-criminal-father. The deepest refutation of the idea of the father as first cause shows that what the family (not just the father) *makes* is "mutual victims." Fictionalized autobiography is a formal structure based on the same truth: it shows "the author" as "the editor," and even as "a character" in his own work, just as it shows that the man Hawthorne has behind him a stern "progenitor" and other ancestors. The father is always a child first—this is another way of putting the more philosophical view of the self as an adulterated compound from the beginning, as the object of someone else's making.

The single crime is invisible and unknown, then, not because it is hidden by the criminal (what the Puritans think), but because it is a lie, a false hypothesis. Elsewhere Hawthorne contemplated a kind of fiction that would forgo characters (as the separate entities, or subjects, we usually take them to be) to people the text with conjunctions—"To personify If—But—And—Though & etc." But *The Scarlet Letter*'s description of the self as a conjunction of selves already enacts this idea, without capitulating to a moral relativism that relieves us of all responsibility, and all humanity. I recognize I am subject to what has gone before me, to my history, as a means not of excusing myself and escaping my acts, but of participating in the larger world of shame and guilt that I share with another: "I, the present writer, as their representative, hereby take shame upon myself for their sakes." *I* exist in so far as *I* am a representative of another at another time: I exist in the place of mercy, between times, on the border of myself and another, in fiction. Mercy, the indwelling form of fiction, rewrites the subject as universal representability, as the exemplary man. And I am he.

That mercy is in fact the form of fiction (and not simply its subject or its effect) is especially well dramatized at certain moments when the narrative comes to a brief halt, in a significant meeting of "author" and "character" (terms that are now as loaded as "self" and "other"). In each case Hawthorne's reticence is a sign of the author's hesitation to judge, to publish another's guilt or shame. There is Hawthorne's hesitation to report that the first object of Pearl's consciousness is the scarlet letter ("shall we say it?"); and his blush at recording (in a recognition of the power of words and their potential criminality) Dimmesdale's scandalous impulse to teach the children wicked words; and his refusal to describe the central revelation of the scarlet letter ("But it were irreverent to describe that revelation");

and his modesty about speaking what Hester cannot reveal to herself—namely, an undiminished love for Dimmesdale ("It might be, too,—doubtless it was so, although she hid the secret from herself, . . . —it might be," where he shifts back and forth between certainty and doubt, for Hester's sake); and even his eschewing to spell out "adultery" anywhere in the text, to fix and publish its meaning; and generally his hesitation to reveal feelings and events "which we have faintly hinted at, but forborne to picture forth"—in this instance, the minister's midnight vigil, where Hawthorne seems almost to have the vision of the minister's pain forced out of himself: "nay, why should we not speak it?" Hawthorne seems under a double obligation (to defend his characters and to inform his reader) that is difficult to reconcile: "[to] hesitate to reveal" and "to hold nothing back from the reader." Silence again and again seems the proper mode of response, even while the story dramatizes a criminal silence—the refusal to name oneself, to recognize one's family, to confess. "It is scarcely decorous, however, to speak all, even when we speak impersonally." It is a crime to speak and not to speak—a riddle that only fiction can begin to solve because, like no other writing, it has as its goal to reveal and to conceal. The foregoing moments of narrative self-consciousness suggest the conjunction of selves that characterizes fiction: where the author hesitates or refuses to write about his characters, I feel I know him best, and see his sympathies most clearly—he gives himself away. In his mercy for his characters he is most himself. It makes mercy no less generous to admit that its teacher can be self-consciousness, and perhaps even narcissism. The pain of speaking autobiographically in "The Custom-House" leads to moral delicacy in the tale. Both author and reader see themselves in the mirror of character, of another, and at the point of painful exposure shrink, and proceed only in the knowledge that in fiction they are defended by seeing themselves in another, by sharing themselves with another, and that in fiction public exposure occurs during the private act of reading. Fiction converts hypocrisy into mercy: what I called, in the first part of this essay, the minister's speaking for and as another, is what the author does in fiction, and what the reader does in reading, as an expression of mercy for himself and another. In this way fiction erases the Puritan interdict, "transgress not beyond the limits of Heaven's mercy!" by taking the terrifying border on which characters live in fear of displacement, in desperate confusion over self and other, and refashioning it into a neutral territory: trespass is converted into sufferance and mercy, the conjunction of selves where we meet.

The minister's voice reaches the same merciful pitch as the author's, when it merges with another's voice because its source is the same—"the same cry of pain." When all else deserts me, pain remains, the surest sign that I have a self: "The only truth, that continued to give Mr. Dimmesdale a real existence on this earth, was the anguish in his inmost soul." Pain substantiates the self not by differentiating it from another's, but by allowing it to see itself in others. In this way Dimmesdale discovers the genuine power of speech and identity: "The burden . . . of crime or anguish . . . kept him down, on a level with the lowest. . . . But this very burden it was, that gave him sympathies so intimate with the sinful brotherhood of mankind; so that his heart vibrated in unison with theirs, and received their pain into itself, and sent its own throb of pain through a thousand other hearts, in gushes of sad, persuasive eloquence." Pain gives Dimmesdale a real existence on earth because it makes him human, part of the brotherhood of mankind; without this human pain, a man "becomes a shadow, or, indeed, ceases to exist." Pain rewrites one's geneology. By insistently pressing how Hester bears her almost unbearable pain ("It was almost intolerable to be borne"; "She had borne . . .", Hawthorne describes her pain as a new birth: "Her sin, her ignominy, were the roots which she had struck into the soil. It was as if a new birth, with stronger assimilations than the first, had converted the forest-land . . . into Hester Prynne's wild and dreary, but life-long home." The new self, like the "new man" Dimmesdale becomes, is born through a crisis in pain that discovers the common heart: "The complaint of a human heart, sorrow-laden, perchance guilty, telling its secret, whether of guilt or sorrow, to the great heart of mankind." What will unlock the secret heart is the call to "be once more human," spoken in a "human language"—the language that the tale has sought from the beginning.

The humanizing power of pain, its ability to replace one's immediate family with "the human family," is the end towards which the tale travels. The discovery of the literal father's identity flows into a larger current of revelation. But to see how the tale's last scene humanizes both father and child, we must first acknowledge that the broken heart can be used as a false sign of humanity, and made an empty symbol. "Not seldom, she [Pearl] would laugh anew, and louder than before, like a thing incapable and unintelligent of human sorrow. Or—but this more rarely happened—she would be convulsed with a rage of grief, and sob out her love for her mother, in broken words, and seem intent on proving that she had a heart, by breaking it." Pearl instinctively knows that sorrow has the capacity to transform her from "a thing," to make her "human." But Hawthorne knows that to be in love with sorrow—a morbid danger both he and his characters court—is merely to find the darker side of narcissism. Pearl requires "a grief that should deeply touch her, and thus humanize . . . her."

Her lack of grief shuts her out even from the brook's melancholy sorrow: " 'If thou hadst a sorrow of thine own, the brook might tell thee of it,' answered her mother, 'even as it is telling me of mine!' " Of course Hester's chiding is unfair: Hester and Dimmesdale rob Pearl of her humanity by not allowing her the grief that is her greatest inheritance. Pearl is cut off from all mankind, then, not simply because she is an unlawful child, but because she has neither sorrow nor sympathy. Pearl becomes human only when she understands her father's words at the end, and sees him "in the crisis of acutest pain." The wild infant is prophesied a woman not simply when she learns who her father is, but when she shares his pain. "The great scene of grief, in which the wild infant bore a part, had developed all her sympathies; and as her tears fell upon her father's cheek, they were the pledge that she would grow up amid human joy and sorrow, nor for ever do battle with the world, but be a woman in it." Neither discovering she has a father nor having the father's name is sufficient to make the child human. Pearl becomes herself when her heart is broken for another. The part she bears in the scene of grief bears her anew. What the child learns from her father is how to realize her own pain through another's. Father and child meet on that common ground where each can say: I now can put myself aside for another, instead of living in terror of being put aside by another.

The kiss Pearl bestows upon Dimmesdale in this last scene unlocks a double mystery. Earlier in the forest Pearl refused the minister a kiss as "talisman" because it was a repetition of the secret passion that begot her. But at the end, in the public marketplace, "Pearl kissed his lips. A spell was broken." Father and child bring each other alive and make readable the ghostly and unintelligible text the other has been. Hawthorne imagines this breaking of a linguistic spell, in another context, for the writer himself: "Here I have made a great blot . . . , a portrait of myself in the mirror of that inkspot. When it reaches thee, it will be nothing but a dull black spot; but now, when I bend over it, there I see myself, as at the bottom of a pool. Thou must not kiss the blot, for the sake of the image it now reflects; though if thou shouldst, it will be a talisman to call me hither again." The pool in which Pearl sees herself reflected becomes, for Hawthorne's own self-reflection, a pool of ink. But the spot of ink, the inviolable circle of self, is transgressed when the reader, in a fictional trespass, offers the talismanic kiss to the text, and reawakens it. The talismanic kiss is offered to the shame we seek to hide (Pearl kisses the scarlet letter in the forest when she refuses to kiss the minister) as the sign of a reader who sympathetically can read the heart almost hidden by *The Scarlet Letter*.

Fiction's most significant accomplishment is not, we see, the thoroughness with which it defends the self, but its ability to keep the self alive and human while defended. This means keeping pain sharp but bounded. The secret power of fiction is pain, publicly expressed and shared, but deflected and bounded in the ways I have shown. Hawthorne describes Hester's decision to bear her pain in order to purify herself as "half a truth, and half a self-delusion"; he hesitantly records (in what I have called his reticent style) her love for Dimmesdale as another source of her decision to remain in the spot of her public ignominy. We think of fiction as such a half truth, half delusion, but the sustained cry of pain in this text leaves almost no room for its farthest fantasy, one that the reader along with the writer hides close beside the secret place of pain—namely, to be "wise . . . not through dusky grief, but the ethereal medium of joy."

Hawthorne's Illegible Letter

Norman Bryson

There are few bodies of writing more intractable to the reader who seeks the continuous production of meaning than the work of Nathaniel Hawthorne, and the fate of that work in critical hands is admirably suited to demonstrate the comedy of intermixed confusion and adulation which writing elevated to "classic" status can expect to encounter. To call a particular work a "classic" may seem harmless enough, but it's a label with a number of less-than-innocent implications. For once a work has been declared to be a "classic," strategies of obscurantism denied the work of low survival-power can at once be mobilised. At its most unarguable level, the designation "classic" means simply that a piece of writing has enjoyed interest over several generations; and while the differing generations are given licence to stress changing and even incompatible aspects of the text as it passes through time, "classic" status serves as a conservative force always able to gather together multiple and divergent readings into a higher unity. For the classic work is agreed to inhabit a realm of inviolable endurance where even the most contradictory interpretation cannot diminish the work's standing. Indeed, for a work to provoke vigorous reaction over a long span testifies to some aloof grandeur whereby the generations may come and go, but the work remains fundamentally unaltered. Two, or several, or many descriptions of the work, however mutually exclusive, none the less are felt to 'bring out' different facets of an ever stronger unity. A critic who is deliberately attacking a prevailing view of a classic work is

From *Teaching the Text.* © 1983 by Norman Bryson. Routledge and Kegan Paul Ltd., 1983.

never in opposition to the coherence of the work itself, only to previous and one-sided readings: the commentary produced will, in the course of time, be placed alongside those it attacked, and the vigour of both readings will serve as proof of literature's superiority to what is written about it. The warring critics will only have released different energies latent in the unified work: multiplicity of interpretation is seen as evidence of immutable grandeur. Moreover, it's often the case that individual critics will attempt, as part of their logistics, to present a self-sufficient reading, one that coheres and produces a seamless fabric of meaning independently of the interpretations already in existence. The task is to yield an interpretation which treats as difficulties to be surmounted, where they are not ignored, moments in the text where continuity appears deficient. And, later, the student encountering manifest discrepancies and discontinuities between critical readings is faced with the often more arduous task of attempting to hold together in the mind critical views which have actually been designed to be untenable together. Reading, now expanded to include criticism, must involve itself in ever more complicated epicycles and adjustments in order to accommodate into a cohesive overview text, critical opinion, and whatever fresh insights that may have been provoked by the work itself. The effort here is one of delicate negotiation which aims always at retrieving unity out of plurality. Classic status demands it: in the power structure of reading, it is the diplomatic incompetence of the reader which is first to be blamed if the desired holism of meaning is not forthcoming, and after that the pugnacity and dogmatism of critics, but only as a last recourse will the classic work itself be queried, to ascertain whether or not the effect of continuous structuration of meaning was intended or not.

With Hawthorne especially the classic designation has, I think, proved disastrous, in that it is often precisely the effect of breaking, tearing, destroying continuous meaning which is the writing's aim. Here I would like to distinguish between three kinds of non-continuous writing: texts which withhold meaning, texts which prevent meaning, texts which destroy meaning. Into the first, "withholding," category would come all those fictions which tantalise the reader with a promise of disclosure always deferred. For example, Faulkner never reveals to us the "true" events which took place in and around Sutpen's Hundred; Pynchon snatches away from us the secret of the contents of Lot 49; and Hawthorne's preacher in "The Minister's Black Veil" takes with him to the grave the meaning of the double fold of black crepe. Into the second, "preventive", category would come Benjamin Constant's *Adolphe*, in which the text itself, Adolphe's confession, lies in a state of becalmed impassivity between the outbursts of interpretation which flank it, the various prefaces and appendices which take up, in relation to the confession, their divergent, impassioned, theatrical attitudes of apology and attack. All Constant's effort in writing the confession, one might say, has been to perfect its dispassion, its deadpan, offering a surface so smooth and resistant that the explanatory missiles aimed at it from both sides will fall back defeated into the outside. And into this category would no doubt also come the purged, ascetic, anti-explanatory writing of Robbe-Grillet; the enterprise of cleansing and erasing human meanings from the world. With both these categories, meaning is a dimension of the text which is absent, posited as occurring in some place where the writing is not, the always elsewhere, in a utopian and veridical history of Sutpen's Hundred, in the pages which would have to tell us about the contents of Lot 49 if the text had not chosen to end with the descent of the auctioneer's hammer, in the secret world the minister inhabits behind the impenetrable veil. Interpretation is what lies either side of, but never within, Adolphe's confession, just as it is the state of affairs prior to Robbe-Grillet's work of effacement or erasure.

The Scarlet Letter differs from these categories in that for the reader the experience of being inside a meaning, inside a guided interpretation, happens all the time. It is not the realm of the off-stage, the prior, or the occulted: the reader is in the thick of it. And by placing the reader in a position where he or she is called upon at all times to be interpreting, explaining, ordering, and from which there is no escape, Hawthorne is able to achieve what these other categories necessarily cannot—to make vivid to the reader the experience of having meanings torn, slashed, destroyed.

Ultimately I want to show this happening at the level of the individual sentence. But an early stage in this disturbing process begins when we ask the unavoidable question: is *The Scarlet Letter* attacking or is it reinforcing the Puritan ethos it describes? Critical argument on this point has produced notoriously conflicting results. If we turn first to the anti-Puritan side, there is of course much evidence suggesting that the novel is a celebration of Hester Prynne's independence, of individual courage against collective cruelty, of the promptings of the heart against social repression. The chapter "The Market Place" shows us the Puritan community as a body of sadistic tormentors, torturing to the point of loss of consciousness a woman Hawthorne intervenes to describe, in a markedly non-Puritan image, as "the image of Divine Maternity . . . the world was only the darker for this woman's beauty, and the more lost for the infant she had borne." Publicly and privately interrogated, Hester heroically refuses to reveal the identity of her lover. Despite the pain of being ostracized, she has the endurance to believe that "the torture of her daily shame would at length . . . work out another purity than that which she had lost; more saint-like, because the result of martyrdom." Over the years, continual acts of charity transform the emblem of her shame into a sign of respect: "They said that it meant Able; so strong was Hester Prynne, with a woman's strength." And in the forest love-scene, Hawthorne states that nothing less than "the sympathy of Nature" supports the lovers' "mystery of joy." As Hester casts away her stigma and removes the cap confining her luxuriant hair, "All at once, as with a smile of heaven, forth burst the sunshine, pouring a very flood into the obscure forest, gladdening each green leaf, transmitting the yellow fallen ones to gold, and gleaming adown the gray trunks of the solemn trees."

That Dimmesdale is unable to withstand the influx of repressed impulses as they emerge into consciousness is, for Hester, a further contingent misfortune. Hester, made strong and self-reliant by her suffering, can cope with the reawakening of her dormant sexuality: that Dimmesdale cannot, that he should move first into crazed submission before the newly released drives, and then into self-consuming sublimation, is only further proof of the dangers of Puritan restraint. Hester can withstand even the final betrayal of her plans by her lover; and in the years after Dimmesdale's death she continues to grow in stature until the scarlet letter "became a type of something to be sorrowed over, and looked upon with awe, yet with reverence too." In her last years, she becomes the legendary comforter and counsellor of distressed womenfolk, the prophet of a time when "the whole relation between man and woman [would be established] on a surer ground."

Such might be the roughest sketch of the anti-Puritan, pro-Hester case. Yet interpenetrating it, almost piercing it, is what one might call, taking the phrase from musicology, its "mirror inversion." For in her solitary cottage by the sea "thoughts visited Hester," Hawthorne tells us, "such as dared to enter no other dwelling in New England; shadowy guests, that would have been as perilous as demons to their entertainer, could they have been so much as knocking at her door": thoughts of murdering Pearl among them. When at last asked by Pearl what the scarlet letter signifies, the supposed paragon of Emersonian self-reliance utters a plain lie—"I wear it for the sake of its gold thread!"; in the process also going back on her promise to Governor Bellingham that the letter would be used as a means of explaining to her daughter the nature of sin. Hester is involved in both social hypocrisy and private deceit, and when Hawthorne darkly states that "The scarlet letter had not done its office," we are given authorial confirmation of a view of Hester strangely at odds with the idea of authentic and courageous rebellion. The Nature that sanctions the lovers' reunion, despite its brief and resplendent flash, is also "that wild, heathen Nature of the forest, never subjugated by human law, nor illuminated by higher truth." And the sense of the lovers' irresponsibility cannot be overlooked when, at the end of the sunlit chapter, we catch sight of Pearl among the creatures of the forest—first the harmless partridges, pigeons and squirrels, but immediately followed by the sinister fox and wolf. Hawthorne is careful to disclaim responsibility for the image of a child abandoned by its parents to be reared by wolves—"here the tale has surely lapsed into the improbable"— but once presented to us, the image remains, and with it, accusation that, in abandoning themselves to the flesh, Dimmesdale and Hester are perpetuating the state of social non-being and non-identity which is their legacy to Pearl. Dimmesdale is too deeply enmeshed in guilt to declare himself to be Pearl's father until the end, but throughout the forest scene we are made aware that not the least of the sins of which Hester and Dimmesdale might be accused is gross negligence of Pearl's emotional needs. The couple may rationalise Pearl's horror at Hester's removal of the scarlet letter by their whispered "Children will not abide any, the slightest, change in the accustomed aspect of things that are daily before their eyes," but it is clear that until Dimmesdale tells Pearl, in person, that he is her father, she will continue to be driven to such desperate conclusions as her claim that she was not "made" but plucked off a rosebush, or that a scarlet letter will spontaneously appear on her gown when she grows to womanhood. The moment Dimmesdale makes his public confession, "A spell was broken"; Pearl is able to cry fully human tears, and before long she is married to her European nobleman. But Hester in the forest is either woefully ignorant or willfully dismissive of her daughter's need for social recognition and integration. Whichever way we interpret Hester's attitude, Pearl's disturbed state is sufficient cause for us to doubt whether her mother's self-abandon in the forest is the mature assertion of individual right which the first, anti-Puritan view claimed.

The point to emphasise is that Hawthorne, in presenting us with contradictory views of Hester, is not writing "ambiguously" in any easily recuperable sense. We cannot take the body of our selections which constitute the pro-Puritan text, and that other body of anti-Puritan citations, and superimpose them one upon the other to produce a stereoscopic richness or depth; we cannot just lay the image of Hester as hero over the image of Hester as villain, to yield the plenitude of the "rounded" character. Contradiction between the meanings that gather at the textual place "Hester" is carried, systematically, to the extreme point where a kind of textual fission begins to take place.

The work of reading may seem at first to lie in fusing the two texts and the two Hesters into a "complex" unity. And if Hester could be isolated from the novel, seen and analysed independently, perhaps this might be achieved. But the same duplicity or breaking of the characterology extends itself like a chain reaction throughout the novel's cast. Let us take the case of Chillingworth. There is so much evidence against him that he might seem the least problematic character in the text: guilty of pressuring Hester into marriage before she was experienced enough to recognise the folly of such a match, guilty of desertion, and above all guilty of the cardinal Hawthornian sin of violating the sanctity of a human heart—we might, as readers, feel relieved that at least one figure in the book is as black as he is painted. Yet Hawthorne renders even this much uncertain by relegating the task of condemnation to the group which the reader, from the first scaffold scene, is least happy to be associated with: the prejudiced, super-stitious and crucifying Boston mob.

> A large number—and many of these were persons of such sober
> sense and practical observation, that their opinions would have
> been valuable, in other matters—affirmed that . . . the fire in
> his laboratory had been brought from the lower regions . . .
> that the Reverend Arthur Dimmesdale . . . was haunted either
> by Satan himself, or Satan's emissary.

Insofar as the reader of the first scaffold scene is opposed to the kind of gothic cruelties which characterise the Bostonian imagination, he or she cannot identify with this form of attack: we want Chillingworth con-demned, but not by such a jury and not in this way. And even this is challenged when, in the scene by the shore, Hester forces Chillingworth to recognise the fiend he has become. "It was one of those moments—which sometimes occur only at the interval of years—when a man's moral aspect is faithfully revealed to his minds's eye." Just as the image of an heroic Hester is pierced by its opposite, so Chillingworth, the Puritan as sadist and tormentor, becomes the Puritan as masochist and victim—the sinister presence becomes the pathetic. And once broken, the villainous image of Chillingworth can never wholly be restored. There is, after all, no reason to doubt the claim that without Chillingworth's ministrations Dimmesdale would have long since died. Chillingworth's motive for hold-ing Dimmesdale back from his recantation is arguably a further impulse of charity: all Chillingworth has wanted is that Dimmesdale relieve himself of the private burden of silence, not that he destroy his reputation. And in the Conclusion, Hawthorne intervenes to tell us that "In the spiritual world, the old physician and the minister—mutual victims as they may have been—may, unawares, have found their earthly stock of hatred and antipathy transmuted into golden love."

There is, of course, one dramatic moment in which Hawthorne might have established how it is we are to view Chillingworth: the moment when Chillingworth discovers whatever is or is not "there" on Dimmesdale's breast. But at precisely that moment the writing plunges into gothic darkness:

> With what a ghastly rapture, as it were, too mighty to be expressed only by the eye and features, and therefore bursting forth through the whole ugliness of his figure, and making itself even riotously manifest by the extravagant gestures with which he threw up his arms towards the ceiling, and stamped his foot upon the floor.

In its excess, the writing partakes of precisely that kind of melodramatisation or diabolisation of reality which has led to the persecution of Hester and Pearl; or rather, the style in which Chillingworth is described seems now to emanate from *himself,* not from the author. At exactly the moment when Hawthorne is called upon to finalise the image of Chillingworth—sadistic inquisitor finally reaching the truth, or hallucinating victim of Puritan over-exegesis—he exchanges authorial identity for that of his character. And one can see why this must be. The narrative strategy demands that the two images of Chillingworth be kept distinct. From another part of the text, from what Barthes called the "hermeneutic code," comes a force which makes an equally insistent demand that one or other of the images be confirmed. Meeting at the description of Chillingworth's reaction, the forces start to tear the text apart: to ensure that the policy of apartheid finally wins, Hawthorne sacrifices or relinquishes his own identity.

It might be possible to analyse the same narrative duplicity in the case of Dimmesdale, were it not for a further twist of the narrative screw. On the plane of psychology, Hester, Chillingworth and Dimmesdale hardly lead separate lives at all: feeding off each other's mutually reinforcing weakness and guilt, at times merging telepathically with each other's thoughts, they seem less like three individual cases than a single, symbiotic organism. This unification on the psychological plane has an immediate consequence on the plane of narrative—if it is not the case that psychology of interdependence is the derivate of the narrative aims. For within this enclosed system, difficulties the reader encounters with one character have their immediate repercussions in the ways the other two are to be assessed. Thus, for as long as we view Hester as the hero of an anti-Puritan text, certain consequences follow. The courage with which Hester withstands the pressure to name her lover makes Dimmesdale's failure to confess seem by contrast the basest of crimes, in which cowardice, hypocrisy and betrayal are united. For as long as we feel it possible that the repression of Hester's sexuality is both unjustified and incomplete, and are waiting for a moment of outright rebellion, Dimmesdale's reticence must arouse our impatience, if not our contempt. The meeting between the lovers in the forest then comes as the book's natural climax, and Dimmesdale's cry, "Do I feel joy again. . . . Methought the germ of it was dead in me," is the revitalisation we have been waiting for. Dimmesdale's reversion, beginning with the infantile pranks of "The Minister in a Maze" chapter and continuing through to the volte-face whereby his ungovernable libido is rechannelled into recantation, must then be seen as a falling away from natural grace, a second betrayal of Hester, and worse in that he no longer has the excuse of cowardice.

But if Hester is a villain, the consequences are otherwise. When we recall that her mind has been taught "much amiss" by its phantom counsellors, that her treatment of Pearl is mendacious and negligent, that her plan to escape is—given her lover's condition and temperament—at the least unrealistic, then Dimmesdale's "reversion" at the end is a less culpable affair than it is if our sympathies are with sexual liberation at all costs. For within this perspective, the central drive of the narrative is less the expectation or hope that Dimmesdale will reach a stage of genital maturity, than that he may find in himself the strength to realise that neither a life under Chillingworth's accusing eye, nor a life of flight with Hester can satisfactorily resolve the contradictions of his predicament. Only public confession will suffice, and the narrative may then be seen to culminate not in the "Flood of Sunshine" chapter but in "The Revelation of the A." Hence the book's thrice-repeated scaffold scenes: in the first, Dimmesdale commits his crime of concealment; in the second he tries, through flagellating by moonlight, at the scene of the crime, to atone for his misconduct; in the third he has realised that the root of his conflict is secrecy, and, heroically rejecting the easy escape Hester has arranged, he undoes the crime of silence at the heart of the book.

Hawthorne, in other words, denies us an absolute Dimmesdale, and forces us to recognise his use of a relative fictional method whereby what Dimmesdale is depends on what Hester and Chillingworth are; and if they are broken, fragmented, torn, then so is he. But more is at stake than the coherence of an individual character. For the difficulties the reader encounters now concern the whole shape of the narrative. Are we dealing with a story centred on the drama of erotic liberation, consistently dark, and reaching an interrupted climax in the forest scene? Or is the centre of the novel elsewhere, in Dimmesdale's cowardice, moving in three developing stages from initial crime (concealment), to provisional amendment (quasi-public revelation), to final resolution (full confession)? Answers to such questions are hard to find: the text refuses to select a fixed position, and neither author nor reader can have the satisfaction of giving the text any certain termination, or closure.

But neither is the text simply "open." Perhaps the most exemplary kind of openness is the end of Pynchon's *The Crying of Lot 49*: "Either Oedipa in the orbiting ecstasy of a true paranoia, or a real Tristero." Either conspiracy or insanity: and either way there will be destruction—Oedipa will lose one of these possibilities. But the destruction will occur outside the text. It is not part of reading: hence its painlessness. Again, if one had access to a veridical history of Sutpen's Hundred, all the impassioned interpretations of the people whose lives have been touched by the events there might be construed as waste; but even so the individual acts of interpretation would retain their validity and their power, however divergent they might be from a "true" account. (I will not labour the point that such an account would only be another "version.") In other words, there can be openness without pain.

The effacement of meanings occurs *before* the writing of the Robbe-Grillet text; it is the precondition of its form. The interpretative missiles launched from both sides of Adolphe's confession cannot penetrate its resistant surface. But the reading of *The Scarlet Letter* is a destruction from within. In a retrospective description such as this the narrative strategies can be seen as orderly and completed design. But at the local reading level, at all those numberless moments out of which that retroactive design is built, one experiences not the gradual emergence of pattern, but an ongoing process of tearing or rending the fabric of meaning.

> Such was the sympathy of Nature—that wild, heathen Nature
> of the forest, never subjugated by human law, nor illumined by
> higher truth—with the bliss of these two spirits.

With almost each word the unfolding sentence switches direction, reverses its loyalties; the effect is one of internal war. One image of a character fights with another, one narrative shape fights with another for the possession of the sentence, and the only moments of truce come from sentences whose allegiance is at the same time to all sides and to none: "Be true! Be true! Be true!"

Nor is there any evident rationale for this destruction of the text by itself; and in this respect the work must be placed in a different category from, in particular, the *nouveau roman*, where an ample theoretical justification for withholding a stable position from the reader is an essential accompaniment to, almost a condition of, the practice of writing. Hawthorne's refusal to create stabilised characters, and his denial to the text of evident climax or thematic centre, are crucial sources of interest in the narrative, and yet they remain mysterious. We can, if we choose—though the argument is hard to sustain—attempt to "close" the "openness" by claiming that "closure" is the pandemic disease of the Puritan society the book is out to attack. Thus, the instances of premature or prejudiced judgment whereby the Hawthorne villain immutably places or fixes a fellow human being can be seen as the central negative act which the whole rhetoric of the fiction seeks to undermine. Hester and Bellingham trying to decide whether Pearl is an angelic or diabolic agent; the community withholding from Hester and Pearl any identity except that typified by the scarlet letter; Chillingworth relentlessly probing the recesses of Dimmesdale's consciousness with the single and exclusive purpose of ascertaining guilt or innocence—all are involved in Manichean ethical judgments which, whether the verdict be positive or negative, remain confined within the most rigid and reductive of frameworks. And it may be that Hawthorne's motivation in the writing of *The Scarlet Letter* was based on the intuition that the reading act is suspiciously, dangerously, similar to this kind of thinking. Denial of fixed characterology, thematic centrality or clear climaxing *may* thus be an ethical choice on Hawthorne's part: perhaps even a strategy whereby Hawthorne could expiate his sense of complicity in the cruelty of his inherited culture, by rendering impossible precisely that kind of judgmental activity which was its most conspicuous and rebarbative characteristic.

While the desire for such self-distancing from a dark inheritance may to some degree account for Hawthorne's calculated uncertainties, the writing will go to such extremes to achieve a state of inner nescience—the radical refusal of the text to supply certain knowledge—that other, and less directly biographical, factors must be looked for. It is reasonably safe to assume that at certain points in the text Hawthorne makes a vigorous claim in favour of the "ontological certainty" of the world, and against those habits of mind which estrange the subject from direct perception of the world's "otherness." No discomfort perplexes Hawthorne's historical placing of the mass hallucinations of the early Puritan community:

Nothing was more common, in those days, than to interpret all meteoric appearances, and other natural phenomena, that occurred with less regularity than the rise and set of sun and moon, as so many revelations from a supernatural source. Thus, a blazing spear, a sword of flame, a bow, or a sheaf of arrows, seen in the midnight sky, prefigures Indian warfare. Pestilence was known to have been foreboded by a shower of crimson light.

No hesitation here menaces a stable distinction between real and imaginary worlds. Yet far more characteristic of the text is Hawthorne's emphatic refusal of description to an innocent or given real. One is partly blinded to the extent of the refusal by the repeated device of alternative interpretation:

> *but whether* it had merely survived out of the stern old wilderness,
> . . . *or whether*, as there is fair authority for believing, it had
> sprung up under the footsteps of the sainted Anne Hutchinson,
> as she entered the prison-door,—*we shall not take upon us to
> determine* [my italics].

The device is beguiling: event, followed by one, two, or three glosses, then the grandiose assertion of the authorial prerogative not to choose from among competing versions. Repeated until it takes on the familiar guise of a stylistic tic, the device assures us of Hawthorne's continuing presence even while it purports to register, among other things, his aloofness and distance from the tale. One hardly notices the deftness of the transition from this fastidious refusal to quibble over details, to the large-scale subversion of the narrative at the level of plot. For, on a small scale, Hawthorne so inoculates us against the expectation of veridical accounts of the real that it is only afterwards, as we cast our mind over the completed shape of the book from the final page, that we feel the shock of realising the extent of the information, crucial to the intelligibility of the story, that has been withheld from us.

Above all, the "A" on Dimmesdale's breast. Since we have already experienced a blurring of this item several times before—the word "adultery" is conspicuously absent from the text, and the initial has been merged with "Able," "Angel"—we are partly anesthetised against the discomfort of never being in a position to know whether Dimmesdale's "A" exists or not. But so much hinges on this question that the text's silence expresses far more than a desire to exploit "the Marvellous." If we were told that Dimmesdale, in an excess of self-punishment, had branded himself with the letter of his shame; if, conversely, we could be certain that Chillingworth's ecstatic revellings before the unbuttoned chest of Dimmesdale had caused a private hallucination; if Hawthorne would side with or against the opposing camps of "eye-witnesses" who both did and did not see an "A" on the dying minister's breast—then maybe we could establish what it in fact is to be an "eye-witness" in Hawthorne's world. The use of fictional uncertainty cannot at this point be rationalised ethically, as might perhaps be argued in the case of Hawthorne's destabilisation of character. Rather, it extends that destabilisation beyond the question of the judgment of individual persons to the larger question of the legibility of the world.

For at its deepest level, *The Scarlet Letter* questions the viability of any narrative within a world where to see is not necessarily to know; where to have the impression of knowing bears an uneasy relation to the evidence of the senses. All of Boston "knows" Hester for an adulterer, even though no one in that community has the least knowledge of any of the circumstances surrounding her adultery; the community similarly "knows" Dimmesdale to be a saint, despite his every protestation from the pulpit to the contrary. Hawthorne will go so far as to present this "knowledge" as false, but hesitates his text on the brink of any alternative truth. That perfect Puritan correspondence between inner state—adultery, and by extension, spiritual preterition—and outward sign—the "A"—can be questioned only by subverting assumptions considered so normal within narrative that quite innocuous passages become tainted with the idea of a duality between inwardness and exteriority:

> A writhing horror twisted itself across his [Chillingworth's] features, like a snake gliding swiftly over them, and making one little pause, with all its wreathed intervolutions in open sight. His face darkened with some powerful emotion, which, nevertheless, he so instantaneously controlled by an effort of his will, that, save at a single moment, its expression might have passed for calmness.

Nothing in this description is firm: Chillingworth's state is not presented from the inside, and all we learn of it is that it is "some" emotion of powerful impact. Yet we cannot go on to examine his outward appearance, since this, too, is unspecified—what does a face that writhes like a snake look like, and how could such a grimace also pass in a trice, for calmness?

The difficulty of understanding the inner state from the outward signs, and the further difficulties resulting from denial of inner/outer correspondence, are typical of what we find in the novel. Hester's strange demonic musings produce no outward trace on her saintly person; Dimmesdale suffers from an inner malaise which is never fully externalised; Chillingworth, demonstrating the obverse of this process, becomes externally the very type of caricature of revenge, yet his motivation may be pure. The darkest, the most disturbing, insight in the book, both for the reader and for the text, is that there may be *no* law of connection between outer and inner worlds. What manifests as intense psychological torture may be the guise of love. A flood of sunshine in a sylvan glade may betoken the depravity of the natural world. Believing that one is far from sanctity may mean that sainthood is burgeoning. The condition Hawthorne presents is one of a deep ignorance of the connections between physical and mental phenomena: we cannot see the world clearly, since we project so intensely on its face; yet even if we do see the world clearly, there is no guarantee that the external appearances before us are stable signs of fixed internal states.

Though this may be an acceptable world-view, one which might, for example, yield a rich poetic literature, it is hard to see how fiction can survive at all under such conditions. For the law of inner/outer correspondence is one of fiction's enabling conventions: the man rubbing his hands and counting piles of coin is a miser; the woman painted an inch thick is a whore; the man who wears yellow gloves and sports an opera hat is a dandy. It is from conventions such as these that fiction grows, qualifying caricature into character, expanding and refining stereotype into psychological and social "truth." Hawthorne retains the outwardness of typology, and even resorts to its crudification. (One problem in the scene of the interview between Hester and Chillingworth on the beach is that Chillingworth has become so exclusively the type of diabolic revenge that he lacks probability, so that the two actors in the scene seem to inhabit the differing and not easily compatible realms of character and caricature.) But simplification of behaviour and appearance is no guarantee that the caricature is, within, as it manifests without.

The peculiarly anti-realist—in the sense of the novel as a record of the real—nature of Hawthorne's art can be emphasised by contrasting his declared fictional intention with that of the European realist programme. "La société française allait être l'historien, je ne devais être que le secrétaire." For Balzac, the act of writing is conceived as an act of transcription of a society whose intelligibility is not in doubt. The world is legible *already*— Balzac even speaks of "Le monde écrit." As each character is introduced, a body of knowledge shared by both author and reader (but it is the author who knows more, whose superior knowledge of the given world the reader desires to possess) will, by reference to physical appearance, to dress, accent, gesture, and the various agreed psychologies of money, love, ambition, age, and so forth, successfully place, with a kind of immutable and self-confident certainty, the exact position in society that a given character occupies. Sollers has described this kind of classic realist fiction as "la manière dont cette société se parle"—the way society speaks itself, as though there were no problematic within the transference of knowledge from society to print, except possible limits to the percipience of the writer. Certainly there is room for ideological commentary—Balzac claimed to be guided by "deux vérités éternelles: la Religion, la Monarchie"—but it is always comment on that which already stands, appendix, to be taken up by the reader as a detachable point of view, a discardable deviation or digression from the overriding task of re-duplication. For George Eliot, the same obliteration of selfhood before an unassailably given reality dominates the process of fiction-making: the texts are presented as the attempt to "give a faithful account of men and things as they have mirrored themselves in my mind."

But with Hawthorne, it is precisely the contract for the transmission of information to a reader who knows much, from a writer who knows more, which is under attack. First, in the opening of "The Custom-House" section, Hawthorne claims that he is not responsible for the text which follows: it is a "mysterious package," wrapped in the scarlet letter itself, with all that entails of fluidity of significance. The "inmost Me," that organising and controlling consciousness which, in the Balzac or George Eliot text, acts to arrange into patterns of intelligibility the data of the world, is kept, Hawthorne rightly warns, behind a "veil." The whole communication of the text, so far from following a model of transmission from A to B, resembles the utterance of the Sybil: the author "casts his leaves upon the wind," sure only that once his production is circulated, its fate will be beyond his control. "Some authors," from whose company Hawthorne excepts himself, imagine that the production of a novel resembles such "confidential depths of revelation as could be fittingly addressed, only and exclusively, to the one heart and mind of perfect sympathy." Intent from the beginning to stress that his text will remain outside the constraints imposed by such intimacy, Hawthorne mocks this approach to fiction: such hopes of a perfect relay of data from author to reader make the mistake of supposing that between the two parties there is a stable contract, a prior relationship, a shared world.

Hawthorne seeks to stimulate or coax the reader into the expectation of such a relationship, but stage by stage its viability recedes. His work operates to render conscious to the reader, and then to subvert and dislocate, the expectation that in a novel, hitherto unknown or misunderstood facts

about a real world will be conveyed from one terminus, replete with information, to another, hungry for information; and that the message will
form a constant, unified structure of meaning. The fiction acts to dislodge
the assumptions and assurances of the realist text; that characters are fixed
enough in essence for us to pass ethical judgments; that external appearance
is the unerring reflection of inward state; that the novel exists to re-duplicate
the pre-established text of the world. If that world-text is illegible, then so
must be the fiction to which it gives rise.

The Prison Door

Evan Carton

The Scarlet Letter is about representation; every major aspect of the novel reflects or re-creates the tension of Hawthorne's representative situation. The subordination of historical event to imaginative construction that the "Legend" progressively effects is *The Scarlet Letter*'s enabling (and constraining) condition. At the outset, its essential and determinative event has already occurred and cannot be recovered by the reader, by the Puritan community, or even by Hester herself. Neither, however, can it be escaped. It can only be represented—multiply, incompletely, transformatively. The "A" is the sign by which the colonial authorities seek to fix the crime and the criminal, but this mark—the alphabet's first letter and its initial—also signifies its own symbolic or representational character, its arbitrariness and its ambiguity. The letter is both limited—no more sufficient to produce in full the never-named adultery than is the magistrates' power to produce both adulterers—and wildly accommodating, susceptible to the multiple readings that begin in the course of Hester's textual history and continue to accumulate throughout her career in criticism. Pearl is another representative of the unpresented original event, but although it is, literally, her origin, she remains an alternative "token," an "emblem," "the scarlet letter in another form." Despite Chillingworth's suggestion that an analysis of her character and mold might reveal the father, she is, like the letter, too elusive or too overwhelming a symbol to yield her source. For the reader and for Hester herself, Pearl's volatile and contradictory significances un-

From *The Rhetoric of American Romance: Dialectic and Identity in Emerson, Dickinson, Poe and Hawthorne*. © 1985 by The Johns Hopkins University Press.

settle the meaning of the generative act; the questions that Pearl is typically and repeatedly asked, however playful or rhetorical they seem, point up her problematic representational status: "Child, what are thou?"; "Canst thou tell me, my child, who made thee?" Finally, the novel's event is encoded in Dimmesdale's conduct and Chillingworth's plot; it is at once obscured and allegorically reenacted in their behavior, and it is represented as well in the interpretive constructions that the letter's readers (both within and without the book) apply.

Hawthorne's representative situation, as it poses the problem of representation itself, not only finds multiple analogues in *The Scarlet Letter* but becomes the crux of the novel. It is a situation that is replicated in the relationship between each principal and the social matrix (the Puritan state remains a matrix, no matter how forbiddingly patriarchal), but its central exemplar is Hester Prynne. Hester is Hawthorne's entry to his Puritan past; her story provides the intimate association with the society of his ancestors that he desires, but it also affords him some distance, for, like Hawthorne, Hester is both a representative and a deviant, a product and a subversive reproducer of her community's meanings. Hawthorne's association with Hester is variously indicated between the moment in "The Custom-House" when the letter first burns on his breast and the moment in the "Conclusion" when he confesses that it still burns in his brain. The simultaneous emergence of Hawthorne from the customs house and Hester from the jail; the "spell" or "fatality" that compels both "to linger around and haunt, ghost-like, the spot where some great and marked event has given color to their lifetime," as if Salem or Boston were "the inevitable center of the universe"; the shared effort to sustain and transform the past through its representation and to win one's proper strength in one's relation to a community—all of these convergences identify the author with his character. But such an identification, as the self-division of both Hawthorne and Hester might suggest, can only be an ambivalent one. Insofar as her enterprise models his, Hester is made to suffer the consequences of the doubt, suspicion, and guilt that attend Hawthorne's acts of imagination; as he censures himself in the voice of his ancestors early in "The Custom-House," so Hawthorne censures Hester in the same representative capacity. If William and John Hathorne distinguish themselves by the persecution of deviant women, their descendant in some sense follows suit. Redemption and repetition often cannot be differentiated in *The Scarlet Letter*'s representations.

The opening words of the story proper are those of the title to Chapter 1, "The Prison Door." Appropriately, Hawthorne's first image suggests the dialectical relations of inner and outer space, solitude and community, bondage and freedom, that generate the novel. Moreover, the uncertain significance (however plain the reference) of the prison door points up the shifting and problematic nature of these relations as their terms harden into mere opposition (the door is a barrier) or collapse into identity (the door is a passage). Here, then, the tension between overdetermination and indeterminacy that informs *The Scarlet Letter* and accounts for much of its power is initiated. Hawthorne enhances this tension in his equivocal treatment of the rosebush and in his assertion that the prison door is "the threshold of our narrative, which is now about to issue from that inauspicious portal." At once assuming a burden of guilt and announcing its release or even its redemption, the narrative proceeds to the marketplace for a scene in which each major character is simultaneously liberated and bound.

The first scaffold scene marks Chillingworth's release by his Indian captors and his entrapment by the spectacular situation that greets him in Boston. More significantly, though, it marks his escape, and Dimmesdale's, from social stigma, from the kind of external determination of personal identity that the community attempts to impose upon Hester. Hester is, ironically, the only potential agent of such determination for both men. "Recognize me not, by word, by sign, by look!" Chillingworth later instructs her, and when she agrees to "keep thy secret, as I have his" she ensures that he, like Dimmesdale, will be able to go unrecognized by the society at large. Paradoxically, however, Dimmesdale's and Chillingworth's apparent avoidance of socially (and historically) determined identities involves more of a loss than a gain of personal autonomy. Both begin to mortify their former selves, to behave compulsively, and to become consumed by their roles as representatives of the society they are deceiving. Hester, on the other hand, suffers ritualized and perpetual public recognition by word, by sign, and by look. Yet such attention invests her with a potential for significance that is not absolutely regulable from without; it engages her in symbolic exchange and thus affords her a vocabulary for self-representation. Like the act that Pearl represents, this vocabulary at once binds and frees, requiring Hester to formulate an identity that resists both detachment from and consumption by it.

In "The Custom-House," Hawthorne first notes his "true position as editor, or very little more" of *The Scarlet Letter*, but later claims to have allowed himself, "in the dressing up of the tale, . . . nearly or altogether as much license as if the facts had been entirely of [his] own invention." Hester's ambivalent relation to her letter mirrors Hawthorne's to his book; she is charged merely with presenting to the public a text that others have determined and authorized, yet in the dressing up of that text she can exercise imaginative license and assume a measure of control over its appearance and meaning. In taking possession of the symbol of her disgrace (and of the disgrace itself), Hester at once realizes and transforms it. It is, in fact, this tension between realization and transformation, obedience and defiance, public and private authority, that produces the shock of Hester's entry into the marketplace:

> On the breast of her gown, in fine red cloth, surrounded with an elaborate embroidery and fantastic flourishes of gold thread, appeared the letter A. It was so artistically done, and with so much fertility and gorgeous luxuriance of fancy, that it had all the effect of a last and fitting decoration to the apparel which she wore; and which was of a splendor in accordance with the taste of the age, but greatly beyond what was allowed by the sumptuary regulations of the colony.

Hester's apparel, "in accordance" with the community's taste yet in violation of its rules, exhibits the mingled compliance and transgression of parody, thus complicating the spectators' understanding of her and, per-haps, of themselves. This wild publication of the letter also reflects the common judgment of Hester's nature, but it constitutes a more aggressive and unsettling confession than the people of Boston had bargained for; its "fertility and gorgeous luxuriance of fancy" suggestively re-create her crime before their transfixed gaze. In short, the "A" on Hester's breast both indicates and thwarts the community's authority over her identity. It makes her "the type of shame"—forces her to "[give] up her individuality" and "become the general symbol at which the preacher and moralist might point, and in which they might vivify and embody their images of woman's frailty and sinful passion," but it also has "the effect of a spell, taking her out of the ordinary relations with humanity, and inclosing her in a sphere by herself." It serves as "the chain . . . of iron links" that keeps her "within the limits of the Puritan settlement" and as "her passport into regions where other women dared not tread" but where "she roamed as freely as the wild Indian in his woods."

The question of control over the letter, and consequently of the sus-ceptibility of Hester's identity to social determination, is most explicitly posed at the end of the long first scene, when the Reverend Mr. Wilson attempts to coerce Hester to name her lover by suggesting that the infor-mation "may avail to take the scarlet letter off [her] breast." Hester's re-sponse is openly revolutionary: "Never. . . . It is too deeply branded. Ye cannot take it off." Taking her punishment more radically to heart than her judges could have anticipated or intended, Hester subverts their sentence by her very faithfulness to it. In so doing, she makes herself the battleground of social and personal authority, of determinate and indeterminate meaning, of letter and spirit. Hester's reply to Wilson out-allegorizes the Puritan magistrates, for if they reduce her to a "type," if they displace her material being by identifying her as "the figure, the body, the reality of sin," she abstracts and displaces the material sign of their allegorical interpretation. Her re-interpretation of the letter does not free her from it or from them, however, but engages her in the play of significances that the magistrates' sentence similarly inaugurates rather than concludes. This is the serious play of the novel, the play on which social order and personal identity are staked and by which each constrains and empowers the other. As Julia Kristeva has noted in another context, "to interpret" means "to be mutually in-debted"; *The Scarlet Letter* observes this definition and rigorously pursues its implications.

In her claim that the letter "is too deeply branded" for the magistrates to remove, Hester acknowledges their power, even internalizes it, while she announces their constraint. The authority she exercises, moreover, binds her as well—a fact that she discovers seven years later when, not in the town but in the forest and not for Puritan law but for romantic love, she finally speaks the name "Arthur Dimmesdale" and briefly imagines that this act can take the scarlet letter off her breast. "The past is gone!" she cries as she discards its mark, echoing Hancock's contention and contra-vening the principle upon which, in "The Custom-House," Hawthorne establishes his novelistic career. Significantly, it is Pearl, alive and at hand, who demands that Hester "take it up" again. For Pearl not only embodies the letter but also enforces its double authorization, identifies it as the product of intercourse, and reveals the limits of Hester's freedom and power. Throughout, Pearl's character and function are those of the letter; she is at once a mutable and ungovernable enigma and—in her repeated demands for explanations of her origin, the letter, and Dimmesdale—a relentless agent of the Puritan order; she represents both Hester's distinction from the community and her connection with it. The extent to which she remains alien to Hester until the novel's final scene is the extent to which she is not "mother's child," as she identifies herself in the governor's hall, but father's—the child of Arthur Dimmesdale, the local minister and rep-resentative of the Puritan patriarchy.

Although Hester vehemently takes Pearl to herself, as she does the letter, she is the independent author of neither, and over neither can she "win the master word." She can only dress them up, "as if [they] had been entirely of [her] own invention." This she does, replicating her initial exhibition of the letter in the ornamentation of her daughter. Hester "bought the richest tissues that could be procured," Hawthorne notes, "and allowed her imaginative faculty its full play in the arrangement and decoration of the dresses which the child wore, before the public eye." Through the play of what Hawthorne repeatedly calls "her art," Hester distinguishes Pearl and herself, indulges the "rich, voluptuous, Oriental characteristic" in her nature, and symbolically asserts her indomitability by the social judgment and strictures that have been imposed on her. Thus, again, she metaphorically reenacts her crime in her needlework: in "the gorgeously beautiful, . . . the exquisite productions of her needle," she finds "a mode of expressing, and therefore soothing, the passion of her life." Yet, if Hester's art preserves her difference, it also constitutes her bond to the Puritan community, for it is the means by which she supports herself and Pearl and participates in communal affairs. This dual significance, in fact, is reflected both in the character of Hester's needlework and in her attitude toward it. The "exquisite productions" in which she takes "pleasure" are set against "coarse garments for the poor," the "rude handiwork" in which "she [offers] up a real sacrifice of enjoyment." Taken as a whole, then, Hester's art comprises both an expression of her passion and an internalization of its punishment, a mode of penance.

It is not simply in her self-mortifying productions, however, that Hester represents, rather than opposing, her society. On the contrary, "deep ruffs, painfully wrought bands, and gorgeously embroidered gloves" are among the most fashionable and lucrative types of her handiwork. "The taste of the age," Hawthorne observes, "demanding whatever was elaborate in compositions of this kind, did not fail to extend its influence over our stern progenitors, who had cast behind them so many fashions which it might seem harder to dispense with." The last clause of this sentence is the crucial one, for it obliges us to ask why embroidery should be an indispensable indulgence for a people that had repudiated so many others. This question and its answer indicate Hester's most profound engagement with the Puritan community.

Embroidery is for the Puritans what it is for Hester: an expression of human presence, human will, human value, a means of laying claim to the world and to oneself. Hence it is "deemed necessary to the official state of men assuming the reins of power," is "a matter of policy" in public ceremonies, is required to "give majesty" to governmental forms, and is "demand[ed]" at funerals "to typify . . . the sorrow of the survivors." Hester's

"curiously embroidered letter," then, the first product of her art, both marks
her sin and her deviance and follows, even epitomizes, Puritan custom: it
is, Hawthorne writes, "a specimen of . . . delicate and imaginative skill,
of which the dames of a court might gladly have availed themselves, *to add
the richer and more spiritual adornment of human ingenuity* to their fabrics of
silk and gold" (emphasis added). More precious than the fabric of experience
itself is the application of a design, the inscription of a purpose, upon it.
The insistence upon such a societal inscription lies at the heart of Puritanism,
as Hawthorne sees it; indeed, Puritanism depends (with magnificent liter-
alness here) on such embroidery as Hester Prynne's. Hester practices the
art of symbolic overlay by which her community gives meaning and distinction to experience, and she suffers from the symbolism that she herself
purveys. Thus, her art—an art that represents not only Hester's passion but
also the Puritans' social enterprise and Hawthorne's literary one—exemplifies her reality and theirs. Material fact in *The Scarlet Letter* is a matter
of embroidery, of "human ingenuity" and "imaginative skill," or perhaps,
as the less salutary meanings of the term would have it, of exaggeration,
fabrication, specious narration.

Hester's intuition of her art's significance—of its constitutive power,
its obliquity, its conduciveness to deception and even self-deception—
prompts her to suspect it and to regard her pleasure in it as a sin. This is
a judgment that, like the embroidery itself, implicates both Puritan reality
and Hawthorne's fiction, and Hawthorne must at once acknowledge and
deflect this implication. Thus the narrator contests Hester's guilty sense of
her art but takes her scruples as a sign of her deviance from clarity and
rectitude: "This morbid meddling of conscience with an immaterial matter
betokened . . . something doubtful, something that might be deeply wrong,
beneath." Embroidery, of course, is not an "immaterial matter," and the
punning play on the notion of materiality here compromises the authority
of the narrator's assertion. Moreover, Hester's imposition of moral significance upon needlework exemplifies the fundamental hermeneutic principle
of her society, a principle that neither she nor Hawthorne is able or willing
to repudiate entirely. The paragraph that precedes the one in which Hester's
judgment is criticized, in fact, suggests several moral explanations for the
popularity of her needlework, explanations that assume and endorse a "morbid meddling of conscience with an immaterial matter" on the part of
Hester's community. ("Vanity, it may be, chose to mortify itself, by putting
on, for ceremonials of pomp and state, the garments that had been wrought
by her sinful hands. . . . But it is not recorded that, in a single instance,
her skill was called in aid to embroider the white veil which was to cover

the pure blushes of a bride. The exception indicated the ever relentless vigor with which society frowned upon her sin." All matters are "material" in Hester Prynne's world; as Hawthorne notes repeatedly during the opening scene of the novel, events that might be dismissed as trivial or taken up as "a theme for jest" by those in "another social state" are "invested with . . . dignity" in Puritan Boston. Yet, it is also true that no matters are material in this world, for all material facts (to paraphrase Emerson) signify (or are "invested with" the significance of) immaterial, or spiritual, facts.

This paradox of material immateriality, or of overdetermined indeterminacy, attends not only the plot elements of *The Scarlet Letter* but also its characterizations. Leslie Fiedler has argued that "one of the major problems involved in reading *The Scarlet Letter* is determining the ontological status of the characters, the sense in which we are being asked to believe in them." As he elaborates this point:

> Hawthorne ends by rendering two of his five main characters (Hester and Dimmesdale) analytically, two ambiguously (Chillingworth and Pearl), and one projectively (Mistress Hibbins). Hester and Dimmesdale are exploited from time to time as "emblems" of psychological or moral states; but they remain rooted always in the world of reality. Chillingworth, on the other hand, makes so magical an entrance and exit that we find it hard to believe in him as merely an aging scholar, who has nearly destroyed himself by attempting to hold together a loveless marriage with a younger woman; while Pearl, though she is presented as the fruit of her mother's sin, seems hardly flesh and blood at all, and Mistress Hibbins is quite inexplicable in naturalistic terms, despite Hawthorne's perfunctory suggestion that she is simply insane.

The importance of Fiedler's analytical and projective modes to an understanding of *The Scarlet Letter*, I would suggest, lies not in the fact that they are constantly opposed in the text but in the fact that their ostensible opposition is constantly collapsing. Fiedler more or less acknowledges as much in his mediatory category of the ambiguous and in his notation of Hawthorne's tendency to reverse or hedge against both analytical and projective characterization. It must be stressed, however, that the problem of characterization is a function not of Hawthorne's vacillating, imprecise, or obscurant use of two different modes but of his challenge to the presumption (ours, as well as the Puritans') that there is any sensible difference between analysis and projection, between the actual and the imaginary. Time and again, in the novel that grows out of his initial analysis (or projection) of "a certain affair of fine red cloth" in "The Custom-House," Hawthorne offers minute analyses of objects, situations, and characters, only to render them projective by contradiction, equivocation, multiplication, or attribution to tradition, to the community, and to his own or even to the reader's fancy. Indeed, the "world of reality" in which Fiedler claims Hester to be rooted is itself, however defined, a projective construct. If it is Hester's social world, it is, ironically enough, the same world that recognizes her only in the allegorical role it projects for her, that of "the type of shame." If it is the world that Hawthorne creates for his readers, it is one in which Hester exists more tangibly than the other characters only by virtue of the narrative's attentive and (for us) appealing psychological projection of her, its insistence on complicating (and modernizing) the Puritan perspective by regularly articulating, as one chapter title puts it, "Another View of Hester."

The Scarlet Letter, then, is always transforming or threatening to transform Fiedler's ontological and epistemological issue into a sociological and linguistic one. We cannot define the status of characters and objects otherwise than as "the sense in which we . . . believe in them," the terms on which we admit them into our thought, our vocabulary, our community. And this sense may be self-serving or self-deluded; these terms may be arbitrary. Puritan Boston affixes a letter to Hester Prynne's breast that identifies her as a type and an outcast and announces the community's own ability to make moral, social, and ontological determinations. But Hester's representative qualities, along with the undiscovered identities of Chillingworth and Dimmesdale, mock this presumption of competence. While she is taken "out of the ordinary relations with humanity," they, as ministers to the townspeople's bodies and souls, are immersed in such relations. The sense in which Chillingworth and Dimmesdale command belief obscures their falsity; the sense in which Hester commands belief obscures her reality. Deviance and representativeness converge in all three, a convergence epitomized in the figure of Mistress Hibbins, the avowed witch and spectral forest denizen who also happens to be Governor Bellingham's sister and the obtrusive sharer of his mansion.

Hawthorne's treatment of Chillingworth sharply illustrates the narrative's general inclination to withhold or unsettle all the bases for absolute moral, social, or ontological judgments. As he first appears, Chillingworth is a classic outsider: old, deformed, oddly dressed, unnaturally intelligent, he stands as a prisoner of the Indians and a still unransomed newcomer to the colony. Soon, however, he has become an agent of social power and justice, strangely reenacting in his private punishment of Dimmesdale the

sentence passed on Hester by the elected magistrates. Rather than condemning Dimmesdale to death, Chillingworth condemns him to live beneath an ever-burning gaze fixed on his breast. Beyond this, the metaphor
that Hawthorne attaches to Chillingworth's retributive enterprise is the
metaphor for the enterprise of Puritan justice. "A blessing on the righteous
Colony of the Massachusetts, where iniquity is dragged out into the sunshine!"cries the town beadle, as he leads Hester to the scaffold. It is another
"inevitable moment," the twin of this one, that Chillingworth seeks—the
moment when his probes, as cautious as those of "a treasure-seeker in a
dark cavern," will strike their object, and "the soul of the sufferer [will] be
dissolved, and flow forth in a dark, but transparent stream, *bringing all its
mysteries into the daylight*" (emphasis added). Both alien and representative
avenger, Chillingworth does also function in the novel's social world as a
healer. "But for my aid, his life would have burned away in torments,
within the first two years after the perpetration of his crime and thine," he
tells Hester, and we are given no cause to doubt his claim.

On his moral function and ontological status Hawthorne provides
conflicting indications. Many of the townspeople "see a providential hand,"
and some enthusiasts proclaim an "absolute miracle," in the timely arrival
of a physician possessed of the skill and devotion to preserve their minister's
failing life. Hester, undeceived at least about his personal identity, early
pronounces: "Thy acts are like mercy. . . . But thy words interpret thee
as a terror!" Yet Dimmesdale's own dying words reverse her judgment
and, interpreting the terror of Chillingworth's acts as a mercy, ratify the
community's initial association of the physician with Divine Providence:
"He hath proved his mercy, most of all in my afflictions. By giving me
this burning torture to bear upon my breast! By sending yonder dark and
terrible old man, to keep the torture always at red-heat!" The narrator, on
the other hand, tends to encourage the reader to view Chillingworth as a
demon, a devil, the Black Man, but deftly undercuts such a view each time
it seems on the verge of confirmation. When Chillingworth, in a paroxysm
of self-recognition, labels himself "a fiend," Hawthorne begins the next
sentence with the words, "the unfortunate physician," and goes on to note
the "look of horror" that accompanied his outburst. In one condemnatory
sentence, Hawthorne modifies "the avenger" with the parenthetical phrase
"poor, forlorn creature that he was, and more wretched than his victim."
And, in Chillingworth's most diabolical scene, when the old man uncovers
the breast of the sleeping minister and celebrates with a grotesque and
riotous dance what he discovers there, Hawthorne refuses to conclude the
chapter with the apparently conclusive satanic association. Instead, gratu-

itously, he adds a sentence that unbalances the equation and reopens to interpretation the issue of Chillingworth's character:

> Had a man seen old Roger Chillingworth, at that moment of his ecstasy, he would have no need to ask how Satan comports himself, when a precious human soul is lost to heaven, and won into his kingdom.
>   But what distinguished the physician's ecstasy from Satan's was the trait of wonder in it!

In his meticulously equivocal last chapter, entitled "Conclusion," Hawthorne catalogues the popular interpretations of Dimmesdale's dying revelation (a revelation not described in the preceding chapter, entitled "The Revelation of the Scarlet Letter"). His list concludes with the testimony of certain "highly respectable witnesses" that there had been no material sign on Dimmesdale's breast, no mark to be viewed, but that "he had made the manner of his death a parable" which required a more abstract reading. The narrator disparages this position on the ground that it resists "proofs, clear as the mid-day sunshine on the scarlet letter." But his phrase, in spite of the certainly of Dimmesdale's guilt, is inescapably ironic. Throughout the novel, light and language have repeatedly proved to be anything but clear, constant, and uncomplicated. The broad daylight of Puritan justice and of Chillingworth's knowledge is, in each instance, compromised by shades of self-deception and darker motives; Hester's letter is openly displayed at the outset but takes on various significances and remains enigmatic to the end. Above all, it is Dimmesdale's identity that is bound up with the complexities of light and language and that is only revealed (insofar as it is revealed at all) by and as their power and their play.

Dimmesdale's first words in the novel are to implore Hester to see "the accountability under which I labor." The accountability is, of course, his obligation as a preacher of the word. But the burden that this role imposes is also its peculiar liberation, much as Hester Prynne's role is one in which bondage and freedom converge. The community requires of—and imposes on—both Hester's letter and Dimmesdale's word a typological significance; in each case it assumes that significance to be exclusively accountable to its interpretive authority, exclusively readable by its lights. But the art of symbolic overlay that Puritan Boston demands and receives from its outcast and its minister is not so easily controlled or interpreted, and the rigidity and predictability of the community's interpretive conventions virtually ensure the duplicity of Hester's and Dimmesdale's "texts." An early example of these conventions, and of the opportunity they afford

Dimmesdale for simultaneously orthodox and subversive ministerial service, occurs in the governor's hall. Pearl, who throughout the book plays with light and even is characterized as the embodiment of the play of light, has just made an unsettling appearance. Her dazzling and freakish attire has shocked the sensibilities of Governor Bellingham and Mr. Wilson, and her perverse response to their religious examination has confirmed them in their decision to remove her from Hester's care. Dimmesdale, at Hester's command, successfully contests this course by offering a symbolic reading of Pearl's offensive appearance and comportment, one that makes conventional Puritan sense of her and relieves Wilson and Bellingham of the confusions of sensory and emotional response. Pearl is to be regarded not as a poorly raised and shamefully dressed child but as God's living judgment upon Hester, a judgment that replicates and ratifies the sentence of the magistrates by combining mercy, retribution, and the opportunity for limited atonement. Pearl is Hester's blessing and her "ever-recurring agony," Dimmesdale asserts, clinching his argument by explaining the child's embroidered gold and crimson tunic typologically: "Hath she not expressed this thought in the garb of the poor child, so forcibly reminding us of that red symbol which sears her bosom?"

Not in material existence but only by the office of the word is faith in a universe of determinate meaning affirmed and renewed; hence Dimmesdale's colleagues give his formulation greater weight than their own experience of Pearl. Because they see the world in figurative terms, the Puritans cultivate the figurative power of language and tailor their interpretive conventions to the discovery (or production) of the broadest significances. But, paradoxically, the very strategies that guarantee meaning, faith, and social order may threaten to undo them. Dimmesdale's duplicitous self-revelations illustrate the point:

> He had told his hearers that he was altogether vile, a viler companion of the vilest, the worst of sinners, an abomination, a thing of unimaginable iniquity; and that the only wonder was, that they did not see his wretched body shrivelled up before their eyes, by the burning wrath of the Almighty! Could there be plainer speech than this? Would not the people start up in their seats, by a simultaneous impulse, and tear him down out of the pulpit which he defiled? Not so, indeed! They heard it all, and did but reverence him the more.

More cynically and guiltily than Hester does, Dimmesdale exploits the difference between his "individuality" and his role as a "general symbol," knowing that his confessions will be interpreted as performances of a symbolic kind. His own self-loathing and his congregation's worship of him thus intensify one another in a vicious spiral that progressively diminishes the possibility of communication as it widens the gap between Dimmesdale's private and public identities. "He had spoken the very truth," Hawthorne notes, "and transformed it into the veriest falsehood."

If he worked his transformations in one direction only, Dimmesdale might be conclusively described as a "subtle, but remorseful, hypocrite." This, however, is not the case, for Dimmesdale not only regularly converts his truth into falsehood but, what is more disturbing, converts his falsehood into truth. Alone among New England divines, we are told, he possesses "the gift that descended upon the chosen disciples at Pentecost, . . . Heaven's last and rarest attestation of their office, the Tongue of Flame." The man whose words contrive to remain universally misunderstood acquires, by virtue of that contrivance, "the power . . . of addressing the whole human brotherhood in the heart's native language"; the man whose inner life is most thoroughly alienated from the world around him acquires through it complete access to that world:

> It kept him down, on a level with the lowest; him, the man of
> ethereal attributes, whose voice the angels might else have listened to and answered! But this very burden it was, that gave
> him sympathies so intimate with the sinful brotherhood of mankind; so that his heart vibrated in unison with theirs, and received
> their pain into itself, and sent its own throb of pain through a
> thousand other hearts, in gushes of sad, pervasive eloquence.

Not only is Dimmesdale's sin inextricable from his saintliness, but the perpetuation of both states depends on the very same quality of his language: its openness to interpretation in the light of its auditor's own needs, desires, assumptions, and experiences. By the same openness he achieves the pernicious and self-serving deceptions of his public "confessions" and conveys the undiscriminating sympathy, the passionate receptivity, that elicits genuine Christian faith and gives him his Tongue of Flame.

Dimmesdale's Tongue of Flame makes him "the mouth-piece of Heaven's messages" in the eyes of his parishioners. For Hawthorne, however, it is more closely aligned with his own duplicitous discourse and with the "hell-fired story" (as he described it to Melville) of *The Scarlet Letter*. The association of Hawthorne's text and Dimmesdale's expression is implicit in "The Interior of a Heart," where Hawthorne not only reports the minister's duplicity but replicates it—and obliges the reader to do the same in his response—by presenting Dimmesdale in two different yet interdependent lights. This association is confirmed in the next chapter, the novel's pivotal chapter and middle scaffold scene, "The Minister's Vigil." Here, too, the elements of light, language, and interpretation dazzlingly intersect, and— more decisively and dangerously than anywhere else in *The Scarlet Letter*— the imaginary and the actual, the deviant and the representative, the false and the true converge.

Dimmesdale's vigil is the desperate product of his mind's "involuntary effort to relieve itself by a kind of lurid playfulness." As a parody of self-exposure, it incorporates both the genuine impulse to confess and its an-tithesis; it "intertwine[s] in the same inextricable knot, the agony of heaven-defying guilt and vain repentance." Throughout the first half of the chapter, material fact and spectral fantasy blend and blur in Dimmesdale's tortured and divided consciousness. But, as the scene continues, the "obscure night," Hawthorne's ambiguous, inconclusive, and contradictory narration, and, finally, events themselves begin to conspire in these convergences. When Pearl, having mounted the scaffold with Hester, asks the minister to "take my hand, and my mother's hand, tomorrow noontide," Dimmesdale an-swers that he shall do so "at the great judgment day," but that "the daylight of this world shall not see our meeting!"

> But, before Mr. Dimmesdale had done speaking, a light gleamed far and wide over all the muffled sky. . . . And there stood the minister, with his hand over his heart; and Hester Prynne, with the embroidered letter glimmering on her bosom; and little Pearl, herself a symbol, and the connecting link between those two. They stood in the noon of that strange and solemn splendor, as if it were the light that is to reveal all secrets, and the daybreak that shall unite all who belong to one another.

Heaven, or Hawthorne's language, here enacts its own bit of "lurid playfulness" which burlesques Dimmesdale's claim. The coincidence of the light and his words seems to reflect a world of immanent meaning, a world capable of confirming and clarifying the human significance intimated in Hawthorne's description of the three linked figures. Yet between the phe-nomenon and its reading stand the words "as if," which are, like the prison door, at once a passage and a barrier. Dimmesdale, as he has done through-out the chapter, insists on producing meaning and takes the light to be a symbolic revelation of his sin. His boundless self-absorption prompts the narrator to issue an extended and vehement refutation:

It was, indeed, a majestic idea, that the destiny of nations should be revealed, in these awful hieroglyphics, on the cope of heaven. . . . But what shall we say, when an individual discovers a revelation, addressed to himself alone, on the same vast sheet of record! In such a case, it could only be the symptom of a highly disordered mental state, when a man, rendered morbidly self-contemplative by long, intense, and secret pain, had extended his egotism over the whole expanse of nature, until the firmament itself should appear no more than a fitting page for his soul's history and fate.

We impute it, therefore, solely to the disease in his own eye and heart, that the minister, looking upward to the zenith, beheld there the appearance of an immense letter,—the letter A,— marked out in lines of dull red light. Not but the meteor may have shown itself at that point, burning duskily through a veil of cloud; but with no such shape as his guilty imagination gave it; or, at least, with so little definiteness, that another's guilt might have seen another symbol in it.

The Scarlet Letter contains few more unequivocal, and no more credible, authorial interjections than this. Not only does the passage differentiate the facts of the narrative from Dimmesdale's fantasies but it affords us the rare security of a normative vantage point from which to judge Dimmesdale's deviant view. It is Hawthorne's interpretative gift to his readers, but two pages later it explodes in their faces. Dimmesdale, on the morning after his vigil, preaches "a discourse which was held to be the richest and most powerful, and the most replete with heavenly influences, that had ever proceeded from his lips," a sermon that brings "more souls than one . . . to the truth." At its conclusion, the sexton closes the chapter by informing the minister of "the portent that was seen last night": "A great red letter in the sky,—the letter A,—which we interpret to stand for Angel. For, as our good Governor Winthrop was made an angel this past night, it was doubtless held fit that there should be some notice thereof!"

That the entire community saw what Dimmesdale saw demolishes the axis of truth and falsity on which we had been evaluating his vision. Indeed, it recasts the phenomenal meteor itself as the multiply and irresolvably interpreted one, the figure, the letter. Beyond their shared perception, the equivalent perceptual behavior of Dimmesdale and the community suggests the minister's representative status at the moment of his wildest perversity.

In embroidering his letter, Dimmesdale, like Hester, may not deviate from the right or even from the conventional so much as he sustains a time-honored interpretive tradition. This view, in fact, finds support in a passage which immediately precedes Hawthorne's dismissal of Dimmesdale's egotistical epiphany:

> We doubt whether any marked event, for good or evil, ever befell New England, from its settlement down to Revolutionary times, of which the inhabitants had not been previously warned by some spectacle of this nature. Not seldom, it had been seen by multitudes. Oftener, however, its credibility rested on the faith of some lonely eye-witness, who beheld the wonder through the colored, magnifying, and distorting medium of his imagination, and shaped it more distinctly in his after-thought.

Private fiction and public history, sinful reverie and divine prophecy, disordered imagination and ordered universe—all are cut from the same cloth, "The Minister's Vigil" implies; gratuitous chance, choice, or power affixes the label.

The Scarlet Letter and the meteor of "The Minister's Vigil" are subversive in the same subtle way: each produces an illumination that unsettles the objectivity of objects by revealing the act of perception that figures in their constitution. The virtual identity between the passage that describes the meteor's effect and the passage in "The Custom-House" that depicts the romancer's atmosphere underlines this relationship:

> It showed the familiar scene of the street, with the distinctness of mid-day, but also with the awfulness that is always imparted to familiar objects by an unaccustomed light. The wooden houses, with their jutting stories and quaint gable-peaks; the door-steps and thresholds, with the early grass springing up about them; the garden-plots, black with freshly turned earth; the wheel-track, little-worn, and, even in the market-place, margined with green on either side;—all were visible, but with a singularity of aspect that seemed to give another moral interpretation to the things of this world than they had ever borne before.

> Moonlight, in a familiar room, falling so white upon the carpet, and showing all its figures so distinctly,—making every object so minutely visible, yet so unlike a morning or noontide visi-

bility,—is a medium the most suitable for a romance-writer to get acquainted with his illusive guests. There is the little domestic scenery of the well-known apartment; the chairs, with each its separate individuality; the centre-table, sustaining a work-basket, a volume or two, and an extinguished lamp; the sofa; the book-case; the picture on the wall;—all these details, so completely seen, are so spiritualized by the unusual light, that they seem to lose their actual substance, and become things of intellect.

I quoted part of the second passage here in [an earlier] discussion of "The Custom-House," in speaking of the self-protective impulse that often prompts Hawthorne to conceal from his readers, and perhaps from himself, the most radical and real implications of his fiction. In that context, I argued that the imputation of insularity and triviality to romance—the suggestion that it can evade or attenuate the pressures of temporality and material circumstance—ignores the dangerous and dynamic engagement with community, time, and physical experience that "The Custom-House" and *The Scarlet Letter* exemplify. By the meteor's light, however, Hawthorne's deceptive characterization of romance begins to appear more revelatory and representative. In "The Minister's Vigil" it is clear that the circumstances of imaginative enterprise are material and the stakes are high. The scaffold is hardly a neutral territory, and, when he ascends to it, Dimmesdale does not leave below his weighty past or his tortured daily life. On the contrary, he seems to draw to him, quite literally, the figures—Hester, Pearl, Chillingworth, Wilson, Bellingham, Hibbins—who dominate or embody both of these realms. The presence of others, moreover, is neither a function of nor a foil for Dimmesdale's imagination. Rather, the entire community shares his visionary experience and takes that experience not as a departure from but as a confirmation of its "actual substance." Thus the cloistered dream pictured in the passage from "The Custom-House" is the social reality of the passage from the novel: like the effects of art, the facts of life are produced by the play of light and the angle of vision and are always subject to "another moral interpretation." Now Hawthorne's prefatory (though composed after the work itself) claim that romance attenuates the most concrete furnishings of actuality and makes them "things of intellect" assumes greater consequence and a different, an anxious, cast. The white light that spiritualizes is the lurid gleam that confounds and consumes.

Hawthorne's own anxiety about his enterprise is succinctly expressed by a writer for the *Church Review* in 1851. *The Scarlet Letter* "saps the foundations of the moral sense," Arthur Cleveland Coxe charged: "We call things by their right names, while the romance never hints the shocking words that belong to its things." Coxe is quite right in his sense that *The Scarlet Letter* challenges a fundamentalist understanding of perception, morality, and language, that it frustrates the attempt to validate them by reference to a reality that exists prior to and independent of their operations. But he misconstrues the force of the challenge and of Hawthorne's book when he implies that its effect is to grant words and thoughts utterly free play in a realm of unencumbered subjectivity. *The Scarlet Letter*'s vision is at once more radical and more conservative than this. If it insists that words and things are not fundamentally joined, it also insists that they cannot be fundamentally disjoined. Such is the equivocal purport of the meteoric letter, that naturalized sign, that conventionalized phenomenon, hurtling through space—a material fact that is no more than a piece of the alphabet, a semantic token that is no less than a piece of the material world. What "The Minister's Vigil" reveals is that the "things of this world" and the "things of [language and] intellect" are neither wholly determinative nor wholly determined; rather, they exist in a relationship of mutual indebtedness. Dimmesdale neither projects the "A" in the sky, as we assume, nor receives it, as he assumes. He interprets it, an act that involves both projection and reception, freedom and constraint. The constraint, moreover, lies not only in the shape of Dimmesdale's object but in the structure of his consciousness, a structure bound to reflect the cultural forms—perceptual, moral, linguistic—of which it is largely composed. Thus, in spying a sign from heaven, Dimmesdale takes his place in the New England tradition of "lonely eye-witness" to divine prophecy; in reading its message as he does, Dimmesdale objectifies the moral principles and psychological pressures of that culture; and in identifying the sign itself as an "A," Dimmesdale sees the same letter that all of Boston sees.

A single mode of expression, even a single token, serves Dimmesdale in his madness, Hester in her defiance, and the society in its orthodoxy. Language enables and enforces their commonality and, in so doing, withholds both determinate reality from Puritan Boston and imaginative indeterminacy from its discontents. At once representative and semantic, language transports history and convention even as it transforms them. This tension manifests itself most elaborately in the lovers' forest rendezvous, a scene that takes place outside of the physical and moral boundaries of society but that Hawthorne wryly introduces in the chapter title, "The Pastor and His Parishioner." Throughout the scene, Hester and Dimmesdale's language sustains and extends the irony of the title. Their transformations—of social identities to natural ones, of religious meanings to romantic ones, of established truths to subversive ones—are always transportations as well; the terms of their escape are the terms of their return.

"Art thou in life?" and "Dost thou yet live?" the lovers ask each other, as if they shared a belief in, and a recollection of, an alternative ontology whose conditions their obvious physical existence would not satisfy. Like "ghost[s]," they glide "back into the shadows of the woods" to redeem themselves by the words they exchange. Variants of the word "truth" appear over and over in their interview. To save Dimmesdale "eternal alienation from the Good and the True," Hester reveals Chillingworth's identity, prefacing her confession with an appeal for forgiveness: "In all things else, I have striven to be true!" When he absolves Hester of sin against their love, Dimmesdale allows himself to re-value his own sinfulness, to forge "another moral interpretation" of his guilt:

> We are not, Hester, the worst sinners in the world. There is one
> worse than the polluted priest! That old man's revenge has been
> blacker than my sin. He has violated, in cold blood, the sanctity
> of a human heart. Thou and I, Hester, never did so!

The reader, who shares in the long-awaited release of tension and who has witnessed only Chillingworth's crime is moved to agree. Yet, theologically, Dimmesdale's is a shocking doctrine. "Thou shalt not violate the sanctity of a human heart" appears nowhere in the Decalogue. It is only a commandment in the gospel of romantic love, toward which the minister has taken a cautious but decided step. Hester's response ratifies his initiative and announces the new dispensation: " 'Never, never!' whispered she. 'What we did had a consecration of its own. We felt it so! We said so to each other!' "

It is a parody of salvation that Hester and Dimmesdale enact in the forest. As sacred language is adapted to profane ends, the relation of pastor to parishioner is also upended. Hester becomes the priestess of romantic love, Dimmesdale her supplicant. "Heaven would show mercy," she pronounces, "hadst thou but the strength to take advantage of it." And she describes to him a new life at whose outset the burdens and stains of this one will melt away:

> Thou art crushed under this seven years' weight of misery. . . .
> But thou shalt leave it all behind thee! . . . Leave this wreck and
> ruin here where it hath happened! Meddle no more with it! Begin
> all anew! . . . Exchange this false life of thine for a true one.

"A Flood of Sunshine" follows, bathing the reconfirmed sinners in the light that they have shunned and that has shunned them throughout. Meanwhile, Hawthorne joins in the production of religious resonances for their halfway covenant. Hester's trials, he tells us, had been "little other than a preparation for this very hour." And of Dimmesdale he remarks: "To this poor pilgrim, on his dreary and desert path, faint, sick, miserable, there appeared a glimpse of human affection and sympathy, a new life, and a true one, in exchange for the heavy doom which he was now expiating." The minister is all but seduced. "O Thou to whom I dare not lift my eyes," he prays, in a final attempt to win some miraculous sanction, "wilt Thou yet pardon me!" But, as the next sentence tersely indicates, the voice he summons and the eyes he meets are Hester's: " 'Thou wilt go!' said Hester calmly, as he met her glance":

> His spirit rose, as it were, with a bound, and attained a nearer prospect of the sky, than throughout all the misery which had kept him grovelling on the earth. Of a deeply religious temperament, there was inevitably something of the devotional in his mood.
>
> "Do I feel joy again?" cried he, wondering at himself. "Methought the germ of it was dead in me! O Hester, thou art my better angel! I seem to have flung myself—sick, sin-stained, and sorrow-blackened—down upon these forest leaves, and to have risen up all made anew, and with new powers to glorify Him that hath been merciful! This is already the better life!"

In his observations on *The Scarlet Letter* Kenneth Dauber points out the revaluation of Puritan language here and reads the scene as a final opportunity for Hester and Dimmesdale to "unite in a universe that is their own extension" and for Hawthorne to establish creative control over his work and intimacy with his audience. "We have, in effect, a series of puns or pun-like structures, alternative definitions of language from which the couple must choose," Dauber writes. The identities of Dimmesdale, Hester, and Hawthorne are doubly committed, however, and in the forest scene the integration of romantic and religious language, like the union of sexual and spiritual passion that initiates the story, suggests that no choice will constitute an adequate basis for self-definition and moral resolution. Still, the characters, author, and critics of *The Scarlet Letter* are subject to the pressure of its dialectics, a pressure so great that it almost seems to validate any decision to relieve it. Hester's injunction to Dimmesdale—"Exchange this false life of thine for a true one"—expresses the necessary presuppositions of such a decision: that the entangled impulses (or meanings) which are implicit in the self-parodic vocabulary of the scene may be separated and objectified as alternative lives, and that these two lives may be accurately identified as a true one and a false one. These presuppositions are incompatible with the complexity that Dimmesdale's character and the novel itself have exhibited up to this point. As critical pitfalls, though, the arbitrariness and partiality of the kind of separation they underlie may be better illustrated by the relationship between two sophisticated and attractive readings of *The Scarlet Letter* that make opposite choices while observing many of the same textual phenomena and, in general sharing a common critical vocabulary. One of these is Dauber's; the other is contained in a recent essay by John Carlos Rowe.

Dauber reads the novel as an attempt to transform a "house of death" into a "house of life," an opportunity for Hawthorne (through the story of Hester) to escape "alienation in the Salem Custom House" by "the reaffirmation of intimacy in Salem terms." The opening chapters are rife with possibility as Hawthorne and Hester take "liberties" with established cultural forms. But the alien form of the Fortunate Fall thwarts their chance for self-renewal and affirmation through creative revision. This typical and external story—Dauber calls it "allegory"—"seizes control, and its dominance is firmly established in the middle of the book." The second half of the novel, Dauber observes, simply copies the first half in a way that schematizes the action and sacrifices the potential of romance to allegory's "predictable end." Rowe also sees in *The Scarlet Letter* "Hawthorne's effort to revivify the static moral categories of Puritanism" by rediscovering "the origins of the communal in the individual." But his Hegelian reading charts a dynamic "transformation of bondage into freedom" through "a narrative that begins with the alienation of the subject from his/her own script and ends with the internalization of language as history." Initially, Rowe argues, "Hester remains fully within the Puritan system of signification" and "is defined also for herself as pure alienation." The first half of the novel, he observes, "perfectly expresses this quality of allegorical externality." Every chapter is "a predicate to the general theological problem of original sin" and the early scenes are mere "allegorical tableaux in which each character plays a predictable role." Conversely, "the second half of *The Scarlet Letter* shifts noticeably into a dramatic, temporalized mode, in which narrative events no longer govern the characters but are determined increasingly by intentional acts."

One measure of the remarkable pitch and poise of the tensions in *The Scarlet Letter* is its capacity to elicit interpretations at once so intimately related and so diametrically opposed as these two. This relationship alone casts an unsettling light on the term that Dauber and Rowe apply differently but understand in the same way, the term that marks the intersection of their arguments: allegory. Both critics define allegory as a form of bondage, a sacrifice of the intimate and internal to the abstract and external, an enforcement of a fixed meaning rather than an engagement in the dynamic or dialectical creation of meanings. In so doing, both imply the distinguishability of (true) experience, or (full, unalienated) selfhood, from its (false, partial, alienated) representation. (This implication, I would argue, is present in both readings in spite of the fact that each critic sees the kind of identity or experience he finds most valid as an achievement of the act of representation.) Their radical divergence on the question of what is allegory in *The Scarlet Letter* and what is not, however, testifies to the novel's implacable resistance to such distinctions. Informed by the structures of language and consciousness, experience is always allegorical, self-divided, at once intimate and abstract, a representation of itself. Its internal difference is, as Emily Dickinson wrote, precisely where the meanings are; that is, the non-identity of its tokens and values both provides for the production of meaning and prevents the absolute establishment of it. In this view, then, allegory, like Hester's letter, is neither submitted to nor overcome. Rather, it is the medium of experience itself, a medium that holds word and thing, spirit and matter, self and other in mutual indebtedness but not in synthesis. As Jonathan Arac has suggested, Hawthorne's use of the allegorical form exemplifies Walter Benjamin's idea that "allegory does not so much enforce any particular meaning as raise the problem of meaning."

Meaning could hardly be more problematic than it is in the concluding chapters of *The Scarlet Letter*. The authorial discomfort that Dauber takes as evidence of Hawthorne's creative frustration by allegory's "final fixing" might be ascribed, at least as convincingly, to Hawthorne's anxiety about the phenomenal inconclusiveness or the moral obliquity of his tale. Rowe's staggeringly sanguine pronouncement that "Dimmesdale's sermon and his confession on the scaffold bring the evanescence of individual self-consciousness into relation with the more enduring values of a social order in which the individual may discover an active, creative role" disregards Hawthorne's uneasiness altogether, as it does the equivocal response that the minister's last performance elicits from Hester and the community alike. Moreover, Rowe ignores the multiple ironies with which Hawthorne laces his description of Dimmesdale's ministerial "triumph," ironies that, as Frederick C. Crews has argued, raise the possibility that the election sermon is the ultimate sublimation of the minister's rekindled passion, that it "is attributable not to Dimmesdale's holiness but to his libido." Indeed, the sermon may be variously characterized, for the crucial fact about it is that it is entirely the product of our characterizations. The novel's climactic piece of language is unwritten and unread. We apprehend it, if at all, only as Hester does, outside "the sacred edifice" and nearer the pillory: "Hester Prynne listened with such intentness, and sympathized so intimately, that the sermon had throughout a meaning for her, entirely apart from its indistinguishable words." The garbled sermon can only communicate "in a tongue native to the human heart"; thus Hester can take it to express her heart's desire. And, in fact, she does understand the sermon and feel its "passion and pathos" in the context of her expectation of imminent reunion with Dimmesdale, an expectation that will soon prove to be a delusion.

When Hawthorne does announce the text of Dimmesdale's sermon, his language is diffident and vague, and the information he offers only draws our attention to the information he withholds: "His subject, it appeared, had been the relation between the Deity and the communities of mankind, with a special reference to the New England which they were here planting in the wilderness." This "relation" is not much clarified by the speech of Dimmesdale's that we do hear, in which his wild self-condemnation as "the one sinner of the world" and his repeated insistence that God's direct and personal attention had all along been focused on the issue of his burning stigma uncomfortably recall the obsessive self-involvement of his midnight trip to the scaffold. Perhaps, too, his cool rebuff of Hester's last hopeful appeal demonstrates spiritual abstraction rather than detached and defensive insularity. In any case, Hawthorne's earlier remark about Hester's deliberate public displays of her letter is an equally apt commentary on Dimmesdale's first and last display of his: "This might be pride, but was so like humility, that it produced all the softening influence of the latter quality on the public mind."

Realization and its parody are balanced in *The Scarlet Letter*'s final scene as they have been in so many earlier ones. The almost comically qualified moral that Hawthorne appends to his tale merely punctuates its ambiguity:

> Among many morals which press upon us from the poor minister's miserable experience, we put only this into a sentence:—"Be true! Be true! Be true! Show freely to the world, if not your worst, yet some trait whereby the worst may be inferred!"

It is not only for the people of Boston, or for Hawthorne's readers, that the truth or falsity of Dimmesdale's salvation remains inferential. The minister, too, can proclaim himself divinely rescued from Chillingworth and yet, in the next moment, turn to Hester "with an expression of doubt and anxiety in his eyes." Questions of meaning and agency persist about the parable that Dimmesdale acts out with a peculiar mixture of willful effort and entranced compulsion. As he nears the scaffold, Hawthorne compares his movement to "the wavering effort of an infant, with its mother's arms in view, outstretched to tempt him forward." It is a disconcerting image: it offers wavering infancy at the moment of Dimmesdale's manly resolve, the mother's enticement at the moment of his reconciliation to the Father's power, prepubescent sexuality at the moment of his confession to adultery, an emblem of pure affection qualified by the charged and unexpected verb "to tempt." Above all, the image objectifies a state of ontological ambivalence; it suspends a moment in which dependence and independence exist in intimate relation and precarious opposition—a moment that allows a glimpse of the complex texture of freedom and bondage that is human identity.

Hester's will, too, like Dimmesdale's and God's, is placed explicitly at issue in this scene in terms that recall her first description and prefigure her last. When Dimmesdale invites her to the scaffold, Hester goes "slowly, as if impelled by inevitable fate, and against her strongest will." These steps repeat and invert the ones taken seven years and two hundred pages earlier, when, at the prison door, Hester repelled the beadle's inevitable hand "by an action marked with natural dignity and force of character, and stepped into the open air as if by her own free will." In each instance, Hester is at once bound and free, self-alienated and self-possessed; in each, a fiction ("as if") at once reveals and conceals the truth. The only reconciliation of these tensions occurs long after both scaffold scenes: "She had returned, therefore, and resumed,—of her own free will, for not the sternest magistrate of that iron period would have imposed it,—resumed the symbol of which we have related so dark a tale." Hester and her community, liberty and compulsion, truth and fiction are resolved equally here by and into an act of representation. The identity that Hester finally wins from the Puritans comprises her decision, "as their representative, hereby [to] take shame upon [herself] for their sakes" and for her own.

Prometheus Ashamed:
The Scarlet Letter
and the Masculinity of Art

Scott Derrick

In their classic studies of nineteenth-century American culture, *Novels, Readers, and Reviewers* and *The Feminization of American Culture*, Nina Baym and Ann Douglas direct our attention to the creation of what might be called a feminized literary marketplace. As female literacy approached 100 percent, and novels appropriated the functions of religious and cultural transmission which had largely been considered to lie within the feminine sphere of interest and influence, women became the chief consumers, as well as the most successful writers of fiction. Although this shift in sensibility materially fostered the emergence of literature as a profession, many male writers nonetheless found it as restrictive as it was enabling.

In the early nineteenth century, we must note, the masculine status of art in America was particularly unstable. Divorced politically and culturally from their European heritage, male American writers struggled with a private world which seemed more and more isolated from the intensely masculine, publicly acceptable commercial culture—a culture which offered no support to the artist. As Whittier tellingly lamented:

> Disappointment in a thousand ways has gone over my heart and left it in dust . . . I have placed the goals of my ambitions high— but with the blessings of God it shall be reached. The world has at last breathed into my bosom a portion of its own bitterness, and I now feel as if I would wrestle manfully in the strife of men. If my life is spared, the world shall know me in a loftier capacity than as a *writer of rhymes*.

In a society which increasingly seemed to feel, as Ann Douglas says, that writing was a feminine activity, male literature existed in a gender crisis of intense form.

Given this revisionist perspective, we might expect that the literature of the period, especially that written by struggling male writers, should reflect a gender ambivalence and aggression rooted in the process of writing itself. If we turn to the greatest book of the period, Hawthorne's *The Scarlet Letter*, this is precisely what we find.

Hawthorne wrote an important biographical sketch of Ann Hutchinson which is mentioned too seldom in discussions of his novel. It begins with the following extraordinary tirade:

> We will not look for a living resemblance of Mrs. Hutchinson, though the search might not be altogether fruitless. But there are portentous indications, changes gradually taking place in the habits and feelings of the gentle sex, which seem to threaten our posterity with many of these public women, whereof one was a burden too grievous for our fathers . . . The hastiest glance may show how much of the texture and body of cisatlantic literature is the work of those slender fingers from which only a light and fanciful embroidery has heretofore been required . . . Woman's intellect should never give the tone to that of man; and even her morality is not exactly the material for masculine virtue. As yet, the great body of American women are a domestic race; but when a continuance of ill-judged incitements shall have turned their hearts away from the fireside, there are obvious circumstances which will render female pens more numerous and more prolific than those of men . . . and the ink-stained Amazons will expel their rivals by actual pressure, and petticoats wave triumphantly over all the field . . . Criticism should examine with a stricter, instead of a more indulgent eye, the merits of females at its bar, because they are to justify themselves for an irregularity which men do not commit in appearing there.

Hawthorne's blast contains the classic tactics of nineteenth-century professional men with regard to women. It asserts that women have inferior aptitudes and deficient characters, that they belong in their "proper spheres," and that constituted authority, such as it is, ought to keep them there. It is additionally striking that this is the association that comes to mind in a piece on the model for Hester Prynne. We should be alerted to both the kind and amount of anxiety *The Scarlet Letter* may contain, and be prepared to examine that text in new and original ways.

At the outset of my reading, I should indicate that I take it for granted that the act of interpretation which I perform is not simply a dry exercise in verifying historical hypotheses, but a dynamic exercise which itself is deeply generative: in short, I believe we do learn history from novels, and history of an important kind; the act of interpretation is neither anarchic nor simply narcissistic. Neither do I claim, however, that I am producing the only "true" reading of Hawthorne, one that claims priority over all other avenues of approach. My working assumption is that the literary text is formed and works socially by a principle of condensation, not completely unlike the condensation of a Freudian dream. More complex than a dream, however, the text can produce widely disparate interpretations as an analogue of the process of its creation. Put simply, any socially successful act must be an intersection of a number of cultural systems or meanings. It might of course be argued that this does not constitute a work of art in any special way, which would merely take us to the truth of Shelley's great phrase: all language is a remnant of a great cyclic poem.

Briefly, the anxiety of *The Scarlet Letter* is of a double kind, reflecting a desire that writing should be masculine, but reflecting, simultaneously, a fear that it somehow is irreducibly feminine and comes from feminine sources. As I indicated earlier, such a view has particular causes and manifestations in American literature, and also has its roots deep in the cultural history of the Western World.

In "The Custom-House," Hawthorne displays a typical unease with his choice of vocation: "What is he," murmurs Hawthorne's ancestor, "a writer of storybooks! What kind of business in life . . . may that be." Indeed, it is not only Hawthorne's ancestors who would not appreciate his art; he it utterly unappreciated in the world of the Custom-House itself, a metaphor for the male world of commerce.

> It is a good lesson, though it may be a hard one—for a man
> who had dreamed of literary fame, and of making for himself
> a rank among the world's dignitaries by such means, to step
> aside out of the narrow circle in which his claims are recognized,
> and to find how utterly devoid of significance, beyond that circle,
> all that he achieves, and all that he aims at.

This hierarchy of business over art, however, will be quickly reversed. "A man of thought, fancy, and sensibility," scoffs Hawthorne, "may, at any time, be a man of affairs, if he will only choose to give himself the trouble."

Hawthorne reaffirms the artist's ultimate triumph in the final metaphor of "The Custom-House," one that is filled with a kind of phallic will-to-power, and rises in a steady crescendo to near hysteria:

> It may be, however—O, transporting and triumphant thought!
> That the great grandchildren of the present race may sometime
> think kindly of the scribbler of bygone days, when the antiquary
> of days to come, among the memorable in the town's history,
> shall point out the locality of THE TOWN PUMP.

Unfortunately, despite his thirst for the glory of conventional fame, his imagination will not work in the masculine world, one which woman, "with her tools of magic, the broom and mop", has never entered. The generative power of imagination is feminine throughout *The Scarlet Letter*, and feminine in a social sense: this should be understood as socially constituted, and not as any Jungian anima. The gesture which inspires the novel-writing project, thinly disguised through projection into the past, is an act of female identification. Hawthorne presses an *A* worn by the adulteress to his breast and feels a heat like a "red-hot iron," the explicit transmutation of the feminine into the phallic. The light by which Hawthorne will write is also feminine, the moon, and the scene of writing will be a tranquil domestic setting which seems both feminine and childlike: littering the room are "a child's shoe; the doll, seated in her little wicker carriage; the hobby horse."

The reader has little doubt that Hester is an artist herself. According to Hawthorne, she

> had in her nature a rich, voluptuous, Oriental characteristic—a
> taste for the gorgeously beautiful which save in the exquisite
> productions of her needle, found nothing else, in all the possi-
> bilities of her life, to exercise itself upon. Women derive a plea-
> sure, incomprehensible to the other sex, from the delicate toil
> of the needle.

In the context of the Ann Hutchinson sketch, however, Hester's sewing represents a strategy of containment. Rather than confront the difficulties of creative women in a "male" field such as literature, Hawthorne has Hester labor in a distinctly female field safely removed from male envy or desire: the "incomprehensible" nature of her pleasure operates like a wall of sexual difference. His earlier comment that needlework, in terms of art, is "then, as now, almost the only one within a woman's grasp" is mistaken enough to seem like a fatuous wish. By 1850, even "the hastiest glance" would show the number of women writing articles, novels, and poems, and Hawthorne's own wife, Sophia, was a painter. Moreover, even in the context of Puritan history, Hester represents a diminishment of her historical model. The real Ann Hutchinson actively invaded the male territory of the ministry. Anyone who reads the moving transcripts of her trial can sense her articulateness, intelligence, and wit, as she faces the withering persecution of Boston's intellectual elite. Despite her potential eloquence, Hester is repressed, silent, and co-opted. At book's end she placates women by sublimating her own anger into a vision of Utopian transformation, a transformation which could only be achieved in daily struggles of a kind Hutchinson represents. Hester's *A* has contained her through the nineteenth-century cult of true womanhood, though she plays the part in Puritan garb. It is in mothering, in raising little Pearl, that she discovers her true vocation, one that saves her from the false vocation of political commitment and religious controversy.

Meanwhile, Pearl herself represents a strategy of containment. By displacing Hester's passion to Pearl, Hawthorne can explore the anarchic tendencies of the imagination without seriously challenging the constitution of the state. If Hester were whole, the consequence would be apocalyptic, as it nearly was in the antinomian controversy to begin with and as Hawthorne himself recognizes:

> Had little Pearl never come to her from the spiritual world, it might have been far otherwise. Then, she might have come down to us in history, hand in hand with Ann Hutchinson, as the foundress of a religious sect. She might, and not improbably would, have suffered death from the stern tribunals of the period, for attempting to undermine the foundations of the Puritan establishment. But in the education of her child, the mother's enthusiasm of thought had something to wreak itself upon. Providence, in the person of this little girl, had assigned to Hester's charge the germ and blossom of womanhood, to be cherished and developed amid a host of difficulties. Everything was against her.

Hutchinson began where Hester ends, as a midwife and counsellor of her peers. Hutchinson, herself a mother, did rupture the community, and was exiled from Boston for her troubles and her eloquence. Meanwhile, because of this splitting between Hester and Pearl, the former never speaks and never "scribbles," a not undesirable state of affairs to Hawthorne, in the context of nineteenth-century competition. This reading may seem harsh in light of *The Scarlet Letter*'s general magnificence; we may feel some reluctance to criticize the way in which the author imaginatively reshapes his material; but we should remember that Hawthorne invites this interrogation in his own massive appropriation of history. If Hester diverges from her historical model, what accounts for the difference?

Hester's lover, or competitor, in the reading of *The Scarlet Letter* I am building, is Arthur Dimmesdale, also a feminized figure who seems more the product of Hawthorne's own sentimental age than of the seventeenth century. Dimmesdale simply doesn't seem like a Puritan leader who "stood up for the welfare of the state like a line of cliffs against a tempestuous tide." Among the possible models for Dimmesdale is one relatively contemporary figure suggested by Lewis Simpson: Joseph Stevens Buckminster, the delicate boy-wonder of the early nineteenth-century pulpit who was known for his literary interests. According to Holmes, Buckminster was "the pulpit darling of his day in Boston. The beauty of his person, the perfection of his oratory, the finish of his style, added to the sweetness of his character, made him one of those living idols." One can certainly not neglect the model of John Cotton himself, who is historically linked to Ann Hutchinson much as Dimmesdale is linked to Hester. Although a promoter of the same doctrine as she, Cotton finally betrayed her at her trial, and so should have felt some of Dimmesdale's guilt. Mark Van Doren proposes still a third model from a fragment in Hawthorne's notebooks: Samuel Johnson.

> Dr. Johnson's penance in Uttoxeter Market. A man does penance
> in what might appear to lookers on to be the most glorious and
> triumphal circumstances of his life.

All three sources seem quite likely and may well have contributed a share to the genesis of Dimmesdale's character. In two of the three, a connection between Dimmesdale and literary fame is explicit. Taken in conjunction with the earlier Hawthorne sketch on Hutchinson, the evidence is compelling that literary fame is on Hawthorne's mind.

Dimmesdale's *A*, unlike Hester's, should be seen as enabling to the extent that it results in the procurement of success, via the production of public discourse. The *A* functions for Dimmesdale in a way homologous with its Custom House function for Hawthorne himself: it leads to a speech, writing, creation, and, at least the author hopes, to fame. The letter confers on Dimmesdale a pentecostal gift of passion, which allows him to address his fellow sinners in "the heart's own language," a language which seems related to the feminine, if we remember the dryness and desiccation of the earlier male world. Dimmesdale's feminization, however, equated with sin, shame, secrecy, and guilt, may only be redeemed in terms of a re-masculinizing triumph, a triumph so sublime that it reduces his sin and shame to nullities. This triumph is achieved when he gives the Election Day Sermon.

Written through a passion which has its source in Hester, a passion reawakened in the forest scene in which Hester displays her own latent eloquence, Dimmesdale's sermon achieves not only a religious and artistic triumph, but a political one. He may be said to actualize symbolically an enduring dream of the American artist, by establishing the political centrality of art, gathering the faithful in a victory which is at once masculine and socially transforming, and healing the split between private selves and public roles.

Even Dimmesdale's triumph, however, paradoxically produces a return of that femaleness it is meant to finally transcend. As Chillingworth says, if Dimmesdale's guilt were revealed, his punishment would be "the gallows." He has not assumed the full punishment for his deed and his silence merely by revealing the *A* he has hidden; instead, he has sealed the extent of his identification with women. Lest we think this identification means identity, however, Dimmesdale is simultaneously moved to indicate his masculine difference by asserting—let us say it—that his *A* is bigger than hers:

> Now, at the death hour, he stands up before you! He bids you look again at Hester's Scarlet Letter! He tells you that, with all its mysterious horror, it is but the shadow of what he bears on his own breast.

Dimmesdale's assumption that he has somehow "out-suffered" Hester dazzles chiefly by its arrogance. Hester, however, seems at least partly convinced by these dramas of male guilt. Confined to her own sphere, she surrenders and wins the right to speak, to her equally suffering sisters, a sentimentalized message of acquiescence in a world emptied of men. Dimmesdale's fame is secure: why should he care if she is a better orator than he? Let the sin of my own reading replicate Dimmesdale's own. *The Scarlet Letter* may be read as a powerful Promethean account of the gender struggles of the American male artist.

Chronology

1804   Nathaniel Hathorne (later Hawthorne) born July 4 in Salem, Massachusetts. Both parents are descended from prominent New England families.

1808   Hawthorne's father, a sea captain, dies in Surinam, New Guinea, leaving the family in poverty.

1821–25   Hawthorne attends Bowdoin College. Longfellow and Franklin Pierce are among his classmates. Writes first fiction.

1825–35   Hawthorne returns to Salem and lives in his mother's house, where in seclusion, he trains himself as a writer.

1828   Hawthorne anonymously publishes *Fanshawe: A Tale* at his own expense. He later destroys the manuscript, which is not republished until after his death.

1830   Publishes stories and sketches in periodicals.

1837   The first edition of *Twice-Told Tales*, a collection of previously published stories, published.

1839   Hawthorne engaged to Sophia Peabody.

1839–41   Hawthorne works as a Measurer in the Boston Custom House. Publishes three children's books: *Grandfather's Chair*, *Famous Old People*, and *Liberty Tree*.

1841   Hawthorne lives at Brook Farm, West Roxbury, Massachusetts. Invests more than one thousand dollars in the project but leaves by the end of the year.

1842   Hawthorne marries Sophia Peabody and moves to the Old Manse, Concord, Massachusetts. His neighbors are Emerson, Thoreau, and Margaret Fuller.

1846   *Mosses from an Old Manse*, a collection of previously published stories and sketches with an introductory essay, published.

1846–49   Hawthorne works as Surveyor in the Salem Custom House.

1850   *The Scarlet Letter* published. Hawthorne moves to a farm near Lenox, Massachusetts. Meets Herman Melville.

1851   Hawthorne publishes *The House of the Seven Gables*, *The Snow Image and Other Twice-Told Tales*, and *A Wonder-Book for Girls and Boys*. Moves to West Newton, Massachusetts.

1852   *The Blithedale Romance* and a campaign biography of Franklin Pierce published.

1853   Publishes *Tanglewood Tales*.

1853–57 Hawthorne serves as United States Consul in Liverpool, England.

1857–59 Hawthorne lives in Rome, Florence, and Redcar, England.

1860   *The Marble Faun* published. Hawthorne returns to the United States. During the next four years he begins another romance and at his death leaves four fragments: "Ancestral Footman," *Dr. Grimshawe's Secret*, "Septimus Felton," and "The Dolliver Romance."

1863   *Our Old Home* published.

1864   Hawthorne dies May 19 at Plymouth, New Hampshire. He is buried in Sleepy Hollow Cemetery, Concord, Massachusetts.

Contributors

HAROLD BLOOM, Sterling Professor of the Humanities at Yale University, is the author of *The Anxiety of Influence*, *Poetry and Repression*, and many other volumes of literary criticism. His forthcoming study, *Freud: Transference and Authority*, attempts a full-scale reading of all of Freud's major writings. A MacArthur Prize Fellow, he is general editor of five series of literary criticism published by Chelsea House.

A. N. KAUL is Vice-Chancellor of the University of Delhi, the author of *The American Vision*, and the editor of *Hawthorne: A Collection of Critical Essays*.

MICHAEL J. COLACURCIO is Professor of English at Cornell University. He is the author of two works on Hawthorne, *The Progress of Piety* and *The Province of Piety*.

RICHARD H. BRODHEAD is Professor of English at Yale University. He is the author of *Hawthorne, Melville, and the Novel* and has edited *Faulkner: A Collection of Critical Essays*.

MICHAEL RAGUSSIS is Professor of English at Georgetown University. He is the author of *The Subterfuge of Art: Language and the Romantic Tradition*.

NORMAN BRYSON is Director of Studies in English at King's College, Cambridge. He is the author of *Vision and Painting* and *Word and Image* and the editor, with Susanne Kappeler, of *Teaching the Text*.

EVAN CARTON is Professor of English at the University of Texas and the author of *The Rhetoric of American Romance: Dialectic and Identity in Emerson, Dickinson, Poe and Hawthorne*.

SCOTT DERRICK is Assistant Professor of English at the University of Pennsylvania and is currently working on a study of Hawthorne's fiction.

Bibliography

Abel, Darrel. "Hawthorne's Dimmesdale: Fugitive from Wrath." *Nineteenth-Century Fiction* 11 (1956): 81–105.

Arvin, Newton. *Hawthorne*. Boston: Russell and Russell, 1961.

Austin, Allen. "Satire and Theme in *The Scarlet Letter*." *Philological Quarterly* 41 (1962): 508–11.

Basket, Sam S. "*The* (Complete) *Scarlet Letter*." *College English* 22 (1961): 321–28.

Baym, Nina. *The Shape of Hawthorne's Career*. Ithaca: Cornell University Press, 1976.

Bell, Michael D. *Hawthorne and the Historical Romance of New England*. Princeton: Princeton University Press, 1971.

Bell, Millicent. *Hawthorne's View of the Artist*. Albany: State University of New York Press, 1962.

Bercovitch, Sacvan. *The Puritan Origins of the American Self*. New Haven: Yale University Press, 1975.

Bier, Jesse. "Hawthorne on the Romance: His Prefaces Related and Examined." *Modern Philology* 53 (1955): 17–24.

Brodhead, Richard H. *Hawthorne, Melville, and the Novel*. Chicago: The University of Chicago Press, 1976.

Charvat, William, Roy Harvey Pearce, and Claude M. Simpson, eds. *Hawthorne Centenary Essays*. Columbus: Ohio State University Press, 1964.

Cottom, Daniel. "Hawthorne versus Hester: the Ghostly Dialectic of Romance in *The Scarlet Letter*." *Texas Studies in Literature and Language* 24 (1982): 47–67.

Cox, James M. "*The Scarlet Letter*: Through the Old Manse and the Custom House." *The Virginia Quarterly Review* 51 (1975): 432–47.

Crews, Frederick C. *The Sins of the Fathers*. New York: Oxford University Press, 1966.

Dauber, Kenneth. *Rediscovering Hawthorne*. Princeton: Princeton University Press, 1977.

Dryden, Edgar A. *Nathaniel Hawthorne: The Poetics of Enchantment*. Ithaca: Cornell University Press, 1977.

Durr, Robert Allen. "Hawthorne's Ironic Mode." *New England Quarterly* 30 (1957): 486–95.

Eakin, John Paul. "Hawthorne's Imagination and the Structure of the 'Custom House.' " *American Literature* 43 (1971): 346–58.

Elder, Marjorie J. *Nathaniel Hawthorne, Transcendental Symbolist.* Athens: Ohio State University Press, 1969.

Fairbanks, Henry G. "Sin, Free Will, and 'Pessimism' in Hawthorne." *PMLA* 71 (1956): 975–89.

Feidelson, Charles. *Symbolism and American Literature.* Chicago: The University of Chicago Press, 1953.

Fiedler, Leslie. *Love and Death in the American Novel.* New York: Stein and Day, 1960.

Fogle, Richard H. *Hawthorne's Fiction: The Light and the Dark.* Norman: University of Oklahoma Press, 1952.

Foster, Dennis. "The Embroidered Sin: Confessional Evasion in *The Scarlet Letter.*" *Criticism* 25 (1983): 141–63.

Gerber, John C. *Twentieth-Century Interpretations of* The Scarlet Letter: *A Collection of Critical Essays.* Englewood Cliffs, N. J.: Prentice-Hall, 1968.

Gross, Seymour. "Hawthorne's Moral Realism." *Emerson Society Quarterly* 25 (1961): 11–13.

Holmes, Edward M. "Hawthorne and Romanticism." *New England Quarterly* 33 (1960): 476–88.

Hutner, Gordon. "Secrets and Sympathy in *The Scarlet Letter.*" *Mosaic* 16 (1983): 113–24.

Jacobsen, Richard J. *Hawthorne's Conception of the Creative Process.* Cambridge: Harvard University Press, 1965.

James, Henry. *Hawthorne.* London: Macmillan and Co., 1879.

Johnson, Claudia D. "Hawthorne and Nineteenth-Century Perfectionism." *American Literature* 44 (1972): 585–95.

Kaul, A. N. *The American Vision: Actual and Ideal Society in Nineteenth-Century Fiction.* New Haven: Yale University Press, 1963.

Leavis, Q. D. "Hawthorne as Poet." *Sewanee Review* 59, Part I (Spring 1951): 179–205; Part II (Summer 1951): 426–58.

Lee, A. Robert, ed. *Nathaniel Hawthorne: New Critical Essays.* London: Vision Press, 1982.

Leverenz, David. "Mrs. Hawthorne's Headache: Reading *The Scarlet Letter.*" *Nineteenth-Century Fiction* 37 (1983): 552–75.

Levin, Harry. *The Power of Blackness: Hawthorne, Poe, Melville.* New York: Alfred A. Knopf, 1958.

Lewis, R. W. B. *The American Adam: Innocence, Tragedy, and Tradition in the Nineteenth Century.* Chicago: The University of Chicago Press, 1955.

Lloyd-Smith, Allan Gardner. *Eve Tempted: Writing and Sexuality in Hawthorne's Fiction.* London: Croom Helm, 1984.

Male, Roy R. *Hawthorne's Tragic Vision.* Austin: University of Texas Press, 1957.

Normand, Jean. *Nathaniel Hawthorne: An Approach to an Analysis of Artistic Creation.* Translated by Derek Coltman. Cleveland, Ohio: Press of Case Western Reserve, 1970.

Rowe, John Carlos. "The Internal Conflict of Romantic Narrative: Hegel's *Phenomenology* and Hawthorne's *The Scarlet Letter.*" *MLN* 95 (1980): 1208–14.

Stubbs, John C. *The Pursuit of Form: A Study of Hawthorne and the Romance.* Urbana: University of Illinois Press, 1970.

Turner, Arlin. *Nathaniel Hawthorne: An Introduction and Interpretation*. New York: Barnes and Noble, 1961.

Van Doren, Mark. *Nathaniel Hawthorne*. New York: Viking Press, 1949.

Waggoner, Hyatt. *Hawthorne: A Critical Study*. Rev. ed. Cambridge: Harvard University Press, 1963.

Winters, Yvor. *Maule's Curse*. Norfolk, Conn.: New Directions, 1938.

Ziff, Larzar. "The Ethical Dimension of the 'Custom-House.' " *MLN* 73 (1958): 338–44.

A cknowledgments

"*The Scarlet Letter* and Puritan Ethics" (originally entitled "Nathaniel Hawthorne: Heir and Critic of the Puritan Tradition") by A. N. Kaul from *The American Vision: Actual and Ideal Society in Nineteenth-Century Fiction* by A. N. Kaul, © 1963 by Yale University. Reprinted by permission of Yale University Press.

"Footsteps of Ann Hutchinson: The Context of *The Scarlet Letter*" by Michael J. Colacurcio from *ELH* 39, no. 3 (September 1972), © 1972 by The Johns Hopkins University Press. Reprinted by permission of the publisher.

"Hawthorne by Moonlight" by Richard H. Brodhead from *Hawthorne, Melville, and the Novel* by Richard H. Brodhead, © 1973, 1976 by The University of Chicago. Reprinted by permission of The University of Chicago Press and the author.

"Family Discourse and Fiction in *The Scarlet Letter*" by Michael Ragussis from *ELH* 49, no. 4 (Winter 1982), © 1982 by The Johns Hopkins University Press. Reprinted by permission of the publisher.

"Hawthorne's Illegible Letter" by Norman Bryson from *Teaching the Text* edited by Susanne Kappeler and Norman Bryson, © 1983 by Norman Bryson. Reprinted by permission of Routledge and Kegan Paul Ltd. and the author.

"The Prison Door" by Evan Carton from *The Rhetoric of American Romance: Dialectic and Identity in Emerson, Dickinson, Poe and Hawthorne* by Evan Carton, © 1985 by The Johns Hopkins University Press. Reprinted by permission of the publisher.

"Prometheus Ashamed: *The Scarlet Letter* and the Masculinity of Art" by Scott Derrick, © 1986 by Scott S. Derrick. Published in this volume for the first time. Printed by permission.

Index

9–10; Henry James on, 1–4,
45; narrative technique of, in
The Scarlet Letter, 76–77,
81–95; novelistic career of,
45–58; associated with Hester
Prynne, 72–73, 98, 99–100,
117; attitude of, towards the
Puritans, 9–20, 33–34, 72, 90,
98; theory of romance of
57–58, 113; and the scarlet
letter, 49, 52, 53, 94, 98; self-
criticism of, 46–47;
ambivalence of, about
sexuality, 25–26, 27; as short
story writer, 46–48; attitude
of, towards women, 2, 8,
21–43, 121–27. Works:
American Notebooks, 53; *The
Blithedale Romance,* 2, 12, 55;
"The Custom-House," 46–47,
48–49, 52, 53, 54–55, 70–71,
74, 77, 94, 98, 99, 101, 105,
112–13, 123–24; "The Devil
in Manuscript," 47;
"Egotism," 18; "Endicott and
the Red Cross," 53; *Fanshawe,*
46; "The Gentle Boy," 26–27;
Grandfather's Chair, 24; "The
Haunted Mind," 52; *The
House of the Seven Gables,* 58;
"The Intelligence Office," 56;
"Main Street," 9–10; *The
Marble Faun,* 2; "The
Minister's Black Veil," 18, 35,
42, 82; *Mosses from an Old
Manse,* 46–47, 56; "Mrs.
Hutchinson," 21, 122; "The
New Adam and Eve," 10–11,
13, 56; "The Old Manse," 47,
53, 55; "Rappaccini's
Daughter," 56; *Twice-Told
Tales,* 46–47; "Wakefield,"
53; "Young Goodman
Brown," 12, 35, 42. *See also
Scarlet Letter, The*
Hibbins, Mistress, 104, 105, 113

History: Hawthorne's treatment
of, 26–27, 49–50, 126; *The
Scarlet Letter* and 31–32, 36, 97
House of the Seven Gables, The, 58
Hutchinson, Ann, 91; and
antinomianism, 22–43; John
Cotton and, 24, 29; as model
for Hester Prynne, vii, 7, 8,
21–43, 122, 125–26; attitude
of the Puritans towards,
24–31; and the Quakers,
26–27; sexuality of, 21–31. *See
also* Prynne, Hester
Hypocrisy: of Dimmesdale, 14,
36–43, 109; and fiction, 77; of
the Puritans, 14, 39

Imagination: as feminine power,
124; in Hawthorne's creative
process, 50–58. *See also*
Moonlight
Indians, Hawthorne's compassion
for, 9–10
Individualism, 20; and sexuality,
24–27, 34, 36
"Intelligence Office, The," 56

James, Henry, 8; on Arthur
Dimmesdale, 16; on Ralph
Waldo Emerson, 2–4, 6; on
Hawthorne, 1–4, 45; on *The
Scarlet Letter,* 4; on
Transcendentalism, 2–4
Johnson, Edward, 27–28, 29, 30,
32
Johnson, Samuel, 126

Kaul, A. N., vii

Language: and Arthur
Dimmesdale, 66–68, 107–12,
126–27; function of, in *The
Scarlet Letter,* 114–20; the
Puritans and, 108–9

16–17, 19, 20; as matrix, 98;
Pearl and, 16, 20; Hester
Prynne and, 13, 15–16, 18,
19, 20, 83–85, 100–101, 102,
107, 120
Puritans, the: and allegory, 33–34,
101, 105; attitude of towards
embroidery, 102–4; ethics of,
vii, 9–20, 83–85; Hawthorne's
attitude towards, 9–20, 33–34,
72, 90, 98; attitude of,
towards Ann Hutchinson,
24–31; hypocrisy of, 14, 39;
and language, 108–9; and the
Quakers, 26–27; and
sexuality, 24–31, 35–36; sense
of sin of, 10, 12–13; and
writing, 72–73

Quaker Catherine, 26, 27
Quakers, the, 26–27

Ragussis, Michael, vii
"Rappaccini's Daughter," 56
Repentance, of Hester Prynne,
32–33
Romance: Hawthorne's theory of,
57–58, 113; *The Scarlet Letter*
as, vii, 113–14
Romantic love, 15, 115–16

Scaffold scenes, 88, 99, 110–11,
120
Scarlet letter, the: and Arthur
Dimmesdale, 91–92, 107,
110–12, 114, 126–27; and
fiction, 73–74; Hawthorne
and, 49, 52, 53, 94, 98;
meaning of, 13, 18, 64–66,
69, 84, 97–98, 100–101, 125;
Pearl as the symbol for,
64–66, 67, 73, 97–98, 101,
108, 110; and writing, 73–74.
See also Dimmesdale, Arthur;

Pearl; Prynne, Hester;
Puritans, the
Scarlet Letter, The: as allegory,
117–18; bastardy metaphor in,
28–29, 32; Hawthorne's
method of characterization in,
83–90, 104–7; influence of
Ralph Waldo Emerson on, vii,
6, 84; and history, 31–32, 36,
97; Henry James on, 4;
function of language in,
114–20; mother-daughter
relationship in, 5–8, 34, 35,
62–66, 84–85, 125;
Hawthorne's narrative
technique in, 76–77, 81–95;
parent-child relationship in,
59–80, 85, 120; as romance,
vii, 113–14; sense of sin in, 6,
10, 11–14, 16–17, 33–34, 103;
symbiotic unity of characters
in, 87–90; view of writing in,
72–73. *See also* "Custom-
House, The"; Hawthorne,
Nathaniel
Sexuality: and antinomianism, 34,
43; and Arthur Dimmesdale,
43, 84, 88, 118–19, 127;
Hawthorne's ambivalence
about, 25–26, 27; of Ann
Hutchinson, 21–31; and
individualism, 24–27, 34, 36;
of Hester Prynne, 21–31, 34,
35–36, 84, 88; and the
Puritans, 24–31, 35–36
Silence, 88; effects of, on the
family, 59–71; effects of, on
Pearl, 62–66
Sin, sense of: of Roger
Chillingworth, 6, 14; of
Arthur Dimmesdale, 6, 16–17;
of Ralph Waldo Emerson, 6;
of Hester Prynne, 6, 12,
33–34, 103; of the Puritans,
10, 12–13; in *The Scarlet
Letter*, 6, 10, 11–14, 16–17,
33–34, 103
Symbolism, vs. allegory, 13–14